Books by Bob Greene

The 50-Year Dash   (1997)
Rebound: The Odyssey of Michael Jordan   (1995)
All Summer Long   (1993)
*To Our Children's Children: Preserving Family Histories
   for Generations to Come*   (with D. G. Fulford)   (1993)
Hang Time   (1992)
He Was a Midwestern Boy on His Own   (1991)
*Homecoming: When the Soldiers Returned
   from Vietnam*   (1989)
Be True to Your School   (1987)
Cheeseburgers   (1985)
Good Morning, Merry Sunshine   (1984)
American Beat   (1983)
Bagtime   (with Paul Galloway)   (1977)
Johnny Deadline, Reporter   (1976)
Billion Dollar Baby   (1974)
Running: A Nixon-McGovern Campaign Journal   (1973)
*We Didn't Have None of Them Fat Funky Angels on the Wall
   of Heartbreak Hotel, and Other Reports from
   America*   (1971)

Bob Greene

The 50-Year Dash

The Feelings, Foibles, and Fears of Being Half-a-Century Old

DOUBLEDAY

New York   London   Toronto   Sydney   Auckland

PUBLISHED BY DOUBLEDAY
a division of Bantam Doubleday Dell Publishing Group, Inc.
1540 Broadway, New York, New York 10036

DOUBLEDAY and the portrayal of an anchor with a dolphin
are trademarks of Doubleday, a division of
Bantam Doubleday Dell Publishing Group, Inc.

Library of Congress Cataloging-in-Publication Data

Greene, Bob.
The 50-year dash / Bob Greene.—1st ed.
        p.   cm.
1. Middle age.   2. Middle aged persons.
I. Title.
HQ1059.4.G74   1997
305.24′4—dc20   96-38920
CIP

For Mark E. Goodman

Contents

The 50-Year Dash

1

Like a Teenager Who's Been in a Fight

A man I've known for years was asked, as he approached 50, whether he really felt middle-aged. He thought about it for a few seconds, and then he answered:

"No. I feel like a teenager who's been in a fight."

So it seems to be for all of us. As 50 rolls around—and, between now and the year 2014, 77 million of us in the United States will turn 50—we enter that strange land that once seemed so far away. Now that it's us instead of some-one else, though—now that it's not our parents who are the 50-year-olds—it's increasingly difficult to fit ourselves into the preconceptions we had about all of this. It's not that 50 is any less weird a concept than we thought it might be. It's just that, even though we accept and even at times embrace the state of being 50, what it really makes us feel like is . . .

Well, like a teenager who's been in a fight.

Battered and weary and sometimes confused, a little the

worse for wear but surprisingly eager for the next round; tired and sore and out of sorts, less sure of things than we used to be but also, on occasion, more than a little smarter; tender where it hurts but strong where no one can see, laughing at things that once would have angered us, mildly shocked by what we see in the mirror but confident that the mirror is not telling the whole story, ready for tomorrow because we know all too well what we've been through today, picking ourselves up and moving in to face the next thump, wherever it may come from, and doing it with a smile, because it's better than the alternative . . .

This is not exactly a guidebook for being 50—it's more like a companion volume to take along on the trip. It's about all the things that 50 is about—family, career, body, money, sex, mortality; friendship, regrets, fears, memories, doubts, dreams; angers, clothes, resentments, houses, parents, fantasies; children, food, love, bosses, doctors, rivalry; yearnings, sleep, employees, shoes, medicine, backaches; hope, cars, lust, embarrassments, heartaches, horizons . . .

It's about 50—the place we never really thought about being, even though we knew we were on our way. Here, at last, we are.

2

Sleepless Nights,
50-Year-Old Feet,
and Other Little Signs

You learn quickly: There are no lightning flashes in the heavens or bold and dramatic messages written across the night sky to let you know what being 50 means.

Instead, the feeling sneaks up on you in tiny ways, like pieces of a jigsaw puzzle you're not all that sure you want to be putting together, but that you can't seem to stop yourself from working on.

Like this:

On Halloween night, without thinking about it, you put a bowl filled with candy outside your door. You do it because you want a little peace and quiet, and don't want to deal with all the kids who come knocking. And as you lock the door after leaving the candy out on the mat, you think: Wait a minute. This must be what a 50-year-old person does.

Or:

You wake up suddenly, and you look at the clock on the

nightstand, and you realize that it's only 1 A.M. No alarm has gone off; no sudden noise has awakened you. The same thing happened to you the night before, and the night before that, and the night before that. It will happen tomorrow night, too. Sleeping through the night, which used to be so routine that you didn't even consider it to be a pleasure, is suddenly the exception. In fact, you can't even remember the last time you slept all the way through the night. You would *kill* to sleep all the way through the night. Looking at the ceiling, you understand, with resignation: This must be how a 50-year-old person sleeps. Or doesn't.

Or this:

You're in Sarasota, Florida, and to the side of the road you see a place called Cars of Yesterday. You remember it as a place that your parents used to take you when you were a child on vacation. You're delighted to see it again. You go inside, expecting to see the cars of yesterday that so enthralled you: the 1910 Model T, the 1923 Pierce-Arrow, the 1911 Waverly Electric. And what you find are . . .

A 1963 Chevrolet. A 1957 Ford. A 1966 Lincoln Continental. The cars of yesterday at today's Cars of Yesterday are cars you remember from your own lifetime. Regular, familiar cars, cars you rode in, cars you drove. They're charging people admission to see these cars now, as if this were a museum. Which, in a way, it is. Why? Because you are 50.

Or this:

You look at your handwriting one day—something you've seen every day for your entire life—and this time instead of just glancing at it, you stop and stare. You think: What is *that*? Your handwriting is sloppy, scratchy, lazy, loose—it appears to be falling apart, disintegrating. You look at it, and you think back to when you were first learning to write script in elementary school, and there is almost no correlation between the careful penmanship of you as a younger person, even of you as a young adult, and this pathetic scrawl on the piece of paper in front of you. You think: Do I have arthritis, or am I going nuts, or what? These words on this piece of paper, you think, were written by a different person than you used to be.

Yet when you receive letters from your oldest friends, or from your parents, their handwriting seems to you to be like their voices, instantly and warmly announcing who has written to you, touching you before you even read the specific words. How can this be? Your own handwriting strikes you as foreign, dissipated, yet theirs is as clear and evocative as their faces. What does this mean?

It means—it must mean—that you are a 50-year-old person. Your friends, you should relievedly know, are occasionally puzzled by the changes they think they perceive in their own handwriting, too—but when your friends see your handwriting, they can still see you, you as a kid, you as they've always known you, standing in front of them.

They're 50, too. That's what all of this means, to you and to them. And it announces itself in all of these small, insistent ways.

Those announcements often don't have their full impact on you until some time after they have occurred. Then you realize what has happened.

An instance from my own recent experience:

I had been staying in a hotel on business, and from upstairs there was a loud, almost constant banging on the floor. I'd been in the same hotel room for several days, and this hadn't happened before. I assumed the noise must be coming from guests who had just checked into the room above mine.

It didn't stop, and it was so loud that I wasn't able to get my work done. I considered calling the front desk and ask-

ing the clerk on duty to look into it, but then I figured: No
need to do that. I'm a reasonable person; I'm sure the guest
upstairs is a reasonable person, too. I'll just dial room-to-
room and, in a pleasant way, explain the noise problem.

I dialed the room number—I knew the room would have
the same digits as my room, but one floor higher—and a
man answered. Now I could really hear the banging,
through his telephone receiver. I told him what the problem was.

"I'm sorry," the man said. "My son's bouncing a ball." I
heard him say to his son: "Hey! I told you to stop that!
You're bothering the man downstairs."

I thanked the man, and hung up and went back to my
work. Only a few hours later did I realize:

To that kid upstairs who was no longer allowed to bounce
the ball, I wasn't some pleasant guy, a guy who had gone
through many of the same things the kid was going
through, a guy who had handled an annoying situation rea-
sonably. I—even though the kid had never seen me—was a
crotchety old man. A classic American icon: the crotchety
old man downstairs.

And the thing is, the kid was right.

There are nights when all the food on the menu seems too
rich for you.

Too rich? When did that start? When did you become a
person into whose mind the concept of food being too rich
could ever possibly enter? Food was never too rich before.
Food was just there.

Probably the too-rich-food phenomenon sets in just
about the time the Weather Channel phenomenon sets in.
Sometimes you will be in a restaurant where there is a television set turned on in the bar area. And sometimes the TV
set will be tuned to the Weather Channel.

The younger people in the restaurant will barely even glance at the Weather Channel. The weather evidently is not something they think about. The weather just *is*—it's out there every day, and it's good or it's bad, and they deal with it.

You and your contemporaries, however, stare at the Weather Channel. Those green areas of precipitation—and those red areas of severe storms—are of great concern to you. Look at that bad weather moving this way. Will it be here by tomorrow morning? Am I going to have to shovel the driveway? Should I remember to get the umbrella out?

The satellite weather pictures from space keep filling the screen of the Weather Channel, and the younger people in the restaurant talk cheerily among themselves and have their cocktails and wait for their tables. You and the other people who are 50 and up fix your gazes on the Weather Channel as if the screen contains the most compelling drama since the days of Shakespeare. John Glenn went into space when you were in junior high school, the first American to orbit the Earth, setting the stage for all the space satellites, with all their technology, that would follow. It had seemed so brave and heroic on that day—a man being shot out toward the stratosphere, for the betterment of the future of mankind—and even if you weren't quite sure of the details of how mankind was going to be helped by those satellites, you knew it had to be in some great and vital way.

It turns out that what John Glenn risked his life for was to provide satellites for the Weather Channel in the restaurant bar.

You wonder where John Glenn is on this night, but you think you know. He's watching the Weather Channel.

On a related note:
An appropriate time to sit back and consider what you

are becoming is when you are at home watching the news on your local TV station, and the bright young weather-caster comes onto the screen, and you think grumpily to yourself:

"I liked the old weatherman better."

When you start missing the old weatherman and being resentful that he is gone, you are deep into being 50.

And:

There are nights when you will actually hear yourself clucking as you watch the news.

Out loud. You. Clucking at the news.

It suddenly occurs to you that in the year just past you have bought more refills for prescriptions than you have bought movie tickets.

Aches and pains—that used to be a meaningless phrase with a silly cadence, like pots and pans, or needles and pins—turn out to be literal. Aches ache. Pains cause you pain. There is nothing remotely minor about the concept of aches and pains—the phrase is anything but a joke. All those places in your body that were once just places—your back, your legs (your sinuses, wherever *they* were)—now as often as not feel like fifty miles of bad road. And as bad as you feel when you're really feeling bad, the worst part is the realization that this is probably as good as it's ever going to get.

Those prescription bottles—the ones more plentiful around your house than movie-theater stubs—are as varied and curious-looking as the boxful of bottle caps you used to collect before aches and pains became your loyal compan-ions.

• • •

On the other hand, there are certain benefits that accrue to you.

For example, when you go to the beach or the swimming pool, you no longer have to worry about how you look, because you are invisible. To the young people prancing around in their bikinis and surf jams, you simply are not there. No need to feel self-conscious because you will never be as lithe or as brawny or as well defined as they are. They don't see you. To them, you are like a lounge chair or a towel hamper—part of the atmosphere, present but unnoticed, except that you have less of a useful function than the furniture. They can't sit on you or toss their soiled towels into you.

You look in the mirror and still secretly see Fabian.

Except Fabian, the way you remember him, was not cold all the time. Summer, winter, fall, spring, you always seem to be putting T-shirts and sweaters on. "Is it cold in here?" you find yourself asking family members, as you add another layer of clothes to what you're already wearing.

Not that your life lacks variety. Many times you ask family members, "Is it warm in here?"

Prime-time television, you finally understand, has nothing to do with you. You shouldn't take it personally—it's kind of like the beach: With the exception of a few well-defined areas, prime-time TV is not supposed to be for you. You realize that the most wasted exercise you could possibly indulge in is to pore over the *TV Guide* Fall Preview issue.

You have no idea which shows are on which channels on which nights. The shows whose nights you do know, they keep switching.

• • •

Speaking to a kid, you hear yourself saying, "Penny wise and pound foolish." You say the words as if they are something you have just thought up. Moreover, after the words have left your mouth you realize that when you said them you were not kidding or making fun of yourself. You meant it quite seriously. Penny wise and pound foolish.

You're 50.

And if you look and listen hard enough, some of the small signs of 50 are bathed in an inherent and resonant sweetness.

In a snatch of overheard dialogue between a wife and husband you can find the values and the lessons of a lifetime.

"Layne, will you get me my reading glasses?" she says.

"Get you what?" he says.

"Wait a minute . . . Maybe I've got them here."

He waits for her.

"Yes . . . I've got them," she says.

Every part of that exchange, every emphasized syllable, every patient second—every unspoken assumption—does, in fact, speak, and it has everything to do with the age of the woman and the age of the man, their chronological ages and the age of their time together. "Will you get me my reading glasses?" She, on some level, is a captive of the age of her eyes, and of the limits that come with that. Everything—menus, phone books, newspapers in the morning light—seems at times to be an insolent adversary.

But there is someone present to fend off the adversaries with her. "Layne, will you get me my reading glasses?" Not a ceremony, not a demand. Eight words, said without thinking, with the power of a song.

• • •

On the street, at 50, you receive a smile from an attractive young person of the opposite sex, a person you have never seen before.

You reflexively turn around, looking over your shoulder, searching for the person for whom the smile is intended.

It's not that you feel that you are really 50. In your mind, there are days when you aren't.

But sometimes you look at the backs of your hands. Or you look at your feet. Or you see the knees of a friend—a friend who is your age—who is standing in a pair of shorts across the way.

And those are 50-year-old hands you are looking down at. Those are 50-year-old feet, those feet of yours. The knees of the friend you see are knees that are 50 years old. There is no escaping that.

You, though, at least the invisible parts of you that matter the most, are not necessarily 50. The backs of your hands— they may be 50 years old. That is something you are willing to concede: The hands, yes, are 50-year-old hands. As if you are simply carrying them around for a while—holding on to them for some 50-year-old person who will pick them up any hour now.

You actually hear yourself saying the words: "Hey, they're supposed to be prisons, not country clubs."

You think that maybe a Cadillac is the right choice. You. In a Cadillac.

You go through drawers and cabinets in your home and you find keys—keys that obviously belong to you, keys that in years past unlocked things that you needed to unlock—and you have absolutely no idea what the keys are for. In your closet you find items of clothing—ties if you are a man, shoes if you are a woman—that are frayed and much used, but that you have no recollection of ever having worn.

You are unable to recall, at 50, the telephone numbers of apartments where as a young adult you used to live, and of offices where you used to work. Those numbers, which at one point during your adult years defined your daily existence, now occupy no space at all in your memory. They might as well be the population of India from some seventh-grade geography quiz—something that you once made yourself memorize, but that is now so far removed that you have not the slightest glimmer. If someone were to dig the phone numbers up and write them on a piece of paper for you, you would probably have some hazy recognition that they once may have signified something to you. Maybe.

It's not just the phone numbers from your early jobs that now seem like something from a distant parallel universe. There are other aspects of those early jobs, too.

When I was a beginning 22-year-old reporter, one of my contemporaries—a fellow the same age—was named Doug Woodlock. He was a bright and aggressive young newspaperman, and soon enough he decided that he didn't want to be a bright and aggressive young newspaperman any longer. He went to law school and ended up being a federal judge.

It was difficult enough for me to get used to thinking of this man—a man I used to address as "Hey, Dougie" in the city room—as His Honor. He was still "Hey, Dougie"— once we talked and I asked him where a judge went shopping for robes, which is a logical question but not one you would ever think of posing to a federal judge, unless the federal judge was at one time known to you as "Hey,

Dougie"—but if he was still "Hey, Dougie," he was also, indisputably, U.S. District Court Judge Douglas P. Woodlock.

That took some becoming accustomed to—the knowledge that the kid reporter I once knew was now a judge. But now we move to a new level—which is that he is, or will soon become, not just a federal judge, but a 50-year-old federal judge. That is something that makes you reflect more about yourself than about him—it's similar to the way you can deal with being 50 years old yourself, and sort of push the thought off to the side, but when you go to a family gathering and you run into your little cousin Molly, and your little cousin Molly is 47 years old, it brings you up short. Judge Woodlock is, or will soon be, 50. I think about whether he remembers the phone number of the city desk at the *Chicago Sun-Times*. Me, neither. We used to call it twenty times a day.

You hear someone say, "Isn't this where Rogers' Drugstore used to be?" Or, "Don't they live in the Gareks' old house?" At 50, all the maps inside your mind are marked with used-to-be's. What is there today is not how you define a place. Places that were new to you when you, too, were new now bear invisible signs. The real sign on the hotel may say that it is Stouffer's, but you know it is the Sheraton Cleveland. The real sign on the house may say that the Schottenstein family lives there, but you know the house is Coach Smith's. The real sign on the little restaurant may say that it is Pizza Plaza, but you know that it is the Toddle House. Your world, at 50, is demarcated by all the signs that are no longer there.

Speaking of pizzas:

When you see a city magazine with a cover story rating

the best pizzas in town, you don't have the faintest interest in reading the results of the survey.

But when you see a cover story that promises to rate the best retirement plans, you grab that magazine as if it will fly away if you don't hold onto it for dear life.

On a trip to another city, you see someone in a crowd, and you think: "Isn't that . . . ?" Then you realize that of course it isn't. The person you think you recognize—the person on the street in the strange town—is 25 years old. You had briefly thought that the person was a person you once knew, a person you last saw twenty-five years ago. If you were to see that person today, he or she would not look at all like the person on this street. He or she, encountered by chance on a street in some town today, would be 50 years old. Like you. Not like this person walking down the street on this day, having no idea who you are.

I saw the weekly newspaper from Bexley, Ohio, the small town where I grew up.

On Page One there was a big picture showing sports action from a Bexley High School basketball game. The caption said that Pat Noles was hitting a long jump shot in the district tournament.

Pat Noles is the son of Lynn Greiner, whom I went to high school with. Lynn Greiner was the younger sister of Tim Greiner, one of my best high school friends. In the photo on the front page of the *Bexley News,* Pat Noles was wearing the white Bexley home uniform, which seemed to have changed little in style from the white home uniforms of the winter of 1965. In the picture his face looked like Tim's face; in the picture his face looked like Lynn's face.

Not that he looked like a kid. He looked like what he was—a senior in high school, a senior starter on the Bexley varsity wearing that white uniform. Wearing a white uniform on game night, 18 years old and a senior, and all the symbolism that has always gone with it—being the person inside that uniform on a night like that.

In the picture he was not some young and innocent carbon copy of who we were in 1965. That's how we sometimes tend to think of those who come after us—as very young, too-young people playing parts that rightfully belong to us. In the picture, though, with the senior-year look on his face, he was just about fully grown, at least as fully grown as we thought we were in our senior year. In the picture he had Tim's face—his uncle's face—and when Tim was 18 he knew he was no longer just a kid.

What it means to be 50 is that Pat Noles is 18, and is no longer all that young. In the picture on the front page of the *Bexley News,* the coach of the high school team is kneeling by the bench behind Noles, watching the ball float toward the basket. The coach of the team is Gene Millard. When I was a boy he was the captain of the Ohio State basketball team, and I would watch him play ("Gino! Gino!" his girlfriend, later to become his wife, would call to him from the stands). Within a few years after graduating from Ohio State he was teaching us history at Bexley High School and coaching our basketball team. He coached for more than twenty-five years, and then he retired from the coaching part of his job—but just recently he had decided to give it a try again. So there he was in the newspaper picture, kneeling in front of the bench, hoping that the jump shot taken by Pat Noles—Lynn Greiner's son, Tim Greiner's nephew—will be true.

Everything you could ever want when you are 18 years old is in that picture. One of the things that you don't want when you're launching your jump shot—with your coach behind you, counting on you—is to be 50.

Not that, at 18, such a thought would even enter your mind.

But at 50, you will from time to time see some relatively old people—vital people in their early 70s—and they will look remarkably young to you.

Little signs:

You find yourself saying to someone—trying to dismissively describe semi-ancient American history—"Yeah, well maybe that's the way they did things fifty years ago . . ."

You're trying to come up with a time frame that denotes the distant past. Only after saying the words do you realize that fifty years ago does not mean Herbert Hoover or Woodrow Wilson. Fifty years ago was a time when you were around. Fifty years ago was part of your time. Being 50 years old sounds a lot younger than the concept of "fifty years ago."

Little signs of 50:

You have a friend who actually sings the praises of buying one of those cardboard head-and-shoulders figures that you're supposed to stick in the window of your house with the living room lights turned on when no one's home. He thinks it's a great idea.

3

Pollen Counts, the Fruit Plate, and Hat-Store Memories

Things—products, clothing, household items, food—define this stage in your life in ways you could not have predicted.

There will come a time, at 50, when you will decide you need a new pair of tennis shoes.

So you will go to the 480,000-square-foot athletic superstore looking for a pair of plain white tennis shoes. You will find tennis shoes with swooshes on the sides, tennis shoes with the manufacturer's brand name emblazoned across the backs (they should be paying their customers for the advertising, not the customers paying them, you will think), tennis shoes with orange and blue starbursts all over them, tennis shoes crisscrossed by black support beams, as if the tennis shoes were a skyscraper. You will find tennis shoes with red liquid capsules displayed in their bottoms, you will find tennis shoes with celebrities' faces painted on them, you will find tennis shoes, designed for adults, with cartoon characters smiling off the shoes' tongues.

You will find tennis shoes made of leather, tennis shoes made of NASA-engineered chemical compounds, tennis shoes made of raw silk. You will realize, somewhere along the line, that you are the only person in the superstore who refers to these shoes as tennis shoes.

You will find that, among the 1.2 million pairs of shoes in the superstore, the one kind of shoe they do not carry is a plain white tennis shoe. You will return home without the pair of tennis shoes you had come with the hopes of buying. You will be exhausted.

It will dawn on you that the fruit plate actually does look good.

The waiter, on the other hand, has no idea what is good. In truth, he probably does, but just as you begin to ask him what's good, you realize: He's half your age. You've been eating food all your life. You know more about what you like than he does. Why are you asking *him* what's good? So you don't.

At 50, it occurs to you, it has been several decades since you went shopping for postcards.

Teachers are out on strike, marching a picket line, anger in their faces, and this is something you don't recall from when you were in elementary school—teachers carrying protest signs in front of their students, proclaiming they don't get paid enough. They're probably right—although as you look into the faces of the children, watching them watch their militant and underpaid teachers, you ask yourself what the children are thinking.

You recall the Christmastime tradition of giving your teacher a gaily decorated carton of cigarettes for the holidays. And how there was a time when everyone, at 50, could be presumed to be carrying cigarette lighters in their pockets. A sentence you rarely hear today: "Got a light?" The Zippos are gone from America's pockets, replaced by electronic devices that promise to open your car door before you get there.

Chesterfields for the teacher for Christmas, and, in retrospect, the message they inadvertently sent: "Season's greetings, hope you die."

On every package of food you buy at the grocery store, you know that you will find—in the same typeface, in the same size of type—the number of calories and grams of fat that are in the food inside the package. The government, in recent years, has set the specifications for these labels.

And, you are reluctant to admit to yourself, you study these labels carefully. Sometimes you look at them before you even look at the picture of the food on top of the package. There was a time in your life when the idea of caring at all how many calories were in a piece of bread was inconceivable to you. Now government administrators—many of them the same age as you—have made sure the labels are there to tell you. The standardized typeface is, not by happenstance, of a size that can be easily read by the weakening eyes of a 50-year-old.

This has not made eating a meal any more fun. It has instead made eating a meal feel a little like balancing a checkbook.

And besides—how do they know? How do they know there are 220 calories in that piece of frozen chicken? They don't know. They're making it up.

• • •

One-hour photo developing shops are convenient and efficient. The quality is good, the service is prompt, the price is reasonable.

So why was it more satisfying, as a kid, to come back from a vacation trip with your family, "send the film out"—that was the unvaried phrase—and wait for a week "for the pictures to come back" (the other unvaried phrase)?

Probably just because anticipation is always more potent than instant gratification. The photos themselves, when they came back, were no more evocative than the photos from the one-hour places are now. But during that week of waiting, the vacation trip took on a mythology of its own— you thought about the color of the water in the lake, the look of the wooden sides of the cabin, the clothes the park ranger wore, the sign at the front entrance of the campgrounds. All of those had been aimed at and clicked at by your family's camera—and all were worth the wait, as you settled back into your daily routine and tried to preserve in your head what the trip had been like.

And when the envelope with the photos finally did arrive, for a few seconds before you opened it up you felt the same excitement you'd felt when you'd started out on the trip itself.

It's different when you only wait an hour. Something is gained, but many, more elusive, things are lost.

Also: You are of the generation that, deep down inside, doesn't believe that eyeglasses that are made for you in an hour will help you see as well as eyeglasses that take five or six days to be prepared.

"Do you think this will brighten up my look?"

The man saying those words—a man of 50—was holding

up a bright red sweater for his wife to look at. They were standing in the aisle of a department store.

"You've never worn a red sweater," his wife said.

"I know," he said. "But what do you think?"

She seemed to be weighing the meaning of this. At 50, a bright red sweater, if you see it on a certain day, holds the promise of sparking up a grayness in your life you weren't even fully aware you felt. At 50—on those certain gray days—a bright red sweater in a store tells you that it will inform the world that you are not as tired as you think you look. You never had a thought like this one before—that clothes of a certain vivid color have the potential of being your advocate in a silent debate with the rest of the world as you walk down the street or sit in your office. On those gray days, though, a bright red sweater seems, at least fleetingly, to hold an answer.

"I think if you like it, you should buy it," she said.

He did. With a flower-patterned tie, on sale in the next aisle.

When you see a bottle of liquor now, you can see the whole story ahead. Not that you don't drink—you do. But the sight of the bottle of liquor is like a movie you've seen too many times before. The idea of "going out drinking," or going to a bar by yourself to sit and drink—an idea that used to make a certain sense to you—now seems bizarre. When you see men and women in bars by themselves, drinking to pass the time, you think they may be potentially dangerous.

The old newspaper-business staple of sending a reporter out to get reaction about a big national news event by interviewing people at a local bar seems demented. What kind of people are sitting around a bar in the middle of the day?

The astronauts are orbiting the moon—*let's go to a bar and ask some noontime alcoholics what they think about it.*

You are 50. You know that if you have one too many drinks, people will think not that you're a sloppy drunk, but that you're a pathetic old drunk. There's a difference. One too many drinks at 50 is a lot less attractive than one too many drinks at 25 or 30.

Not that it never happens to you. You know how this movie ends, but once in a while you have the inexplicable desire to go see it again, as if the conclusion will be happier this time.

As far as your expectations of gracious service and personal attention go, the advent of salad bars may have been the beginning of the end.

Not that you ever thought about it when you were younger—but if you had, you wouldn't have believed that at 50 you would be more dependent on batteries than you were as a child.

Batteries for your laptop computer, batteries for your cable-box zapper, batteries for your garage-door opener, batteries for your pocket calculator. Batteries for your wrist-watch, batteries for your cellular phone, batteries for your smoke detector, batteries for your tape player . . .

Your daily battery demand is more capacious than on Christmas morning when you were 8 years old. And while there seemed to be only one or two sizes of batteries back then—the big round ones that went into a flashlight, and the little round ones that went into a toy robot—today you need specialized training to tell the difference between the boundless varieties of batteries. Every time you think you've finally figured out the difference between AA and AAA, they bring out products that require AAAA or AAAAAAA.

It's as if the manufacturers of the world realize they can hook tens of millions of 50-year-olds on batteries more effortlessly than any drug dealer ever hooked a sucker on dope. You will end up, in your lifetime, spending far more on batteries than you ever did on the products they are designed to go into.

And the frustration of putting the tiny batteries into the miniaturized electronic machines in your house is an extra little thwack, engineered by the battery cartel just to make fun of you and humiliate you. They know you're out there. With twenty or thirty sets of batteries wearing out, all at once.

John F. Kennedy, more than any other person, was responsible for the disappearance of the corner hat store.

Before Kennedy's presidency, there were hat stores on the downtown corners of every city. Adams Hats—that, if memory serves, was one of the big chains. They were there because they were necessary—men wore hats, especially downtown when they went to the office, and the hat stores bustled and prospered because the customers kept streaming in.

The unluckiest businessman of all may well have been the one who opened a hat store on Kennedy's Inauguration Day. Kennedy hardly ever wore a hat in public, and because he didn't, American men didn't, either. A nation of 50-year-olds walks by the downtown corners where the hat stores once were, perhaps not even remembering they used to be there. They have been replaced by enterprises selling the new American staples: gourmet coffee and chocolate chip cookies.

The telephone in the house you grew up in—the heavy black phone with the rotary dial—may not have been pretty, but it was a snap to use. Was there a person in the world who didn't understand how to dial a number?

At 50, you find that telephones have been improved to the point where you have no idea what some of the buttons ("flash," "save," "conference," "speed") do. You go to a store and buy a phone (another improvement no one needed—before they improved things, a telephone company worker would come to your house with a phone for you and attach it to the wall and you'd be done), and now when you get it home you realize you have no clue about how to use most of its features, and you probably never will.

It's like the hotel-room alarm clocks with the multiple array of settings: Alarm 1, Alarm 2, buzzer, snooze, sleep, music, auto. With the old alarm clocks, you could go to sleep fairly confident that you would wake up at the time you had selected—all you'd had to do was move the little rotating pointer to halfway between the 6 and the 7, pull the alarm lever out, and you knew you'd be awakened at 6:30. With the Alarm 1, Alarm 2 bedside clocks, you lie awake worrying that you've done it wrong. Which you usually have.

"Would you like some dessert?"

At 50, your answer to that elementary sentence has become a litmus test of whether you're good or bad, a determiner of whether you are a responsible or irresponsible person. From someone who used to deem Fudgsicles and Milk Duds as two of the basic nutritional building blocks, you have become someone who must face every offer of dessert with the conscience of a person poised on a ledge, being taunted into stepping forward by the throngs on the street far below. "Would you like some dessert?" With the implied and unspoken follow-up: "Are you weak and foolish enough, fatso?"

•   •   •

An addendum to the Adams Hats theory:

While the corner hat shops of the 1950s may be gone, today men of 50 and older have taken to wearing baseball caps (bought in the same athletic superstores that don't carry plain white tennis shoes). Whatever it is that baseball caps represent—freedom from care, jauntiness, a footloose attitude on a warm spring day—is what men are in the spiritual market for. Plus, under a baseball cap all scalps are created equal.

It's as if we are trying to convince ourselves that it was the fedoras, and not our fathers and grandfathers beneath them, that made them 50.

The changes of a lifetime evolve gradually, but when exactly did pasta happen?

A piece of advice at 50:

If you come upon an old Rolodex or address book that is thick and filled with important names and phone numbers from earlier in your adult life, do yourself a favor:

Don't read it.

You don't consider yourself mirthless or a stick-in-the-mud, but you could do without the bouquets of balloons that have taken the place of bouquets of flowers.

Also: those greeting cards from which confetti falls onto your lap and onto your floor, making you angry for the rest of the day.

You are an American who grew up with Ford Fairlanes and Chevy Impalas zipping cheerily along the highways and by-ways. You are 50 now, and the steel-reinforced minivans and double-height family-fun trucks around you on your way home from work are like armored tanks rolling down the occupied streets of your memory.

"Let's split it."

In the restaurant the two husbands say the words simultaneously as the check arrives. They and their wives have just completed a dinner out. The men reach into their wallets and toss their American Express cards onto the middle of the table, the two cards meeting in midair and dropping to the tablecloth.

It's a ceremony of middle age—a little clanking of swords in hearty good fellowship as the young waiters and waitresses watch in silent amusement. Flipping the credit cards onto the table with barely a glance at the bill, signaling that it doesn't really matter if one wife had two more glasses of wine than the other, or that one husband had soup and dessert while the other did not.

A sort of tame bravado—it will have to do, at this stage in your life. Errol Flynn and Tyrone Power—*Let the chips fall where they may!*—in a restaurant full of other 50-year-olds tossing cards.

The lure of the Lands' End catalog, and others like it, is a little more complicated than the simple premise of ordering clothes through an 800 number and getting two-day delivery.

Lands' End has turned out to be the way to get rid of the lingering memory of your dad taking you to buy clothes at the big department store downtown. You would stand there with your father looking over your shoulder—you, 11 years old and itchy—and your father would tell the salesman, whom he knew, that you were in the market for your first suit, which you weren't, if it had been up to you.

And the salesman putting jackets on you and pulling

them off and replacing them with other jackets, the tailor making chalk marks near your ankles, you wanting to be out playing with your friends, wanting to be anywhere but here . . .

And most of all, your father yanking a tie up tight against your neck, deciding it was the wrong tie, looping another tie around you while the jackets came and went, the chalk marks were moved up and down, yanking the tie knot even tighter this time, you wishing you were the Great Houdini and could escape from this diabolical trap . . .

Lands' End, forty years later, is the antidote. That's why it's so successful. You look in a catalog. They send you the stuff. If you don't like it, you send it back. No questions asked, no excuses demanded. No hands upon you nor nooses on your spirit.

You ask yourself whether people today would ever go into a bookstore if they couldn't get biscottis, videotapes, compact discs and espresso.

You now live in a world where, at a given moment, you can always be made aware of the wind-chill factor and the pollen count. As with the calories and fat content of the food you buy, having this knowledge available does not make you feel any better than when you lived in a world where no one told you such things. There are times, in fact, when you are convinced that having this knowledge makes you feel a lot worse.

Student stand-by.

That combination of words means nothing now. For a brief period of time, though—the period that encompassed the years when you were a college student—the words stood for a small and self-contained social structure that felt kind of nice, kind of exotic.

The major airlines offered half-price tickets for college students who were willing to wait in a certain area of the airport concourses to see if any seats would become available at the last minute. You had to show a valid college ID card to be a part of this; there were no advance reservations, no way to know if you'd make the flight until just before the doors closed.

All of the students desiring to board all of an airline's flights gathered in the same area—if you made a flight, you'd be sent hurrying to the departure gate. There was something unfettered and informal and festive about the student-stand-by gates at America's airports—friendships were made there during long preholiday afternoons and nights of waiting, romances were begun, stories were exchanged. Even the airline employees who worked at the student-stand-by gates seemed somehow less authoritarian and stiff than the employees at the regular gates.

It all seems very archaic now—like some silly gimmick out of the youthquake/Carnaby Street/luv era of generational self-imagery and marketing. And it must not have been economically sensible, because it went away before long, never to return.

But there are days when you hurry through La Guardia or O'Hare or LAX, on your way to get on a flight that will take you to a business meeting, and you glance over toward a gate and you think you remember it as being the student-stand-by gate of thirty years ago. You'll get your miles on today's flight, and you'll save them for future family vacation trips or first-class upgrade stickers, all a part of the frequent-flier club you're enrolled in—the place where all the student-stand-by fliers have ended up.

•   •   •

Some of life's requirements that were drilled into you early as being so important that you must never forget them seem, at 50, not so essential for you to know. Such as remembering to regularly rotate your tires.

Also, you sense there used to be a lot more concern expended on mufflers and muffler maintenance.

Cologne, once a product that occupied a certain small but omnipresent place in your thoughts, now seems to be something for 15-year-olds.

Rain on the roof—a phrase so soothing that the Lovin' Spoonful turned it into a hit song—has always sounded wonderful: gentle and rhythmic and calm.

So why, at 50, is your first instinct when you hear rain on your roof that the roof may be leaking, and that it's going to be your responsibility to get it fixed?

There are times, at three o'clock in the morning, when you concede that our new national anthem is the car alarm.

Women know this about men, perhaps even better than men know it:

Pants look terrible.

Men's pants—men's dress pants. Even the best men's dress pants look clunky and dumb. At 50, you realize that no pair of pants truly fits or looks good. Men go through their entire adult lives avoiding this conclusion, but if you stop and look at any pair of pants on any man, you know. That's why men like jeans so much—jeans can come close to looking OK (although the chances of this decrease incrementally with each year past 40). A shirt can look OK—a sport coat can look OK. A pair of pants . . . you don't want to think too hard about it.

When the salesclerk says, "That looks good on you," you sense at 50 that he most likely doesn't mean it.

A frightening thought:
Of all the scientific innovations and technological breakthroughs during our time on Earth, the one that may last the longest after we are gone—the one that may still be a part of life 25,000 years from now—is the Frisbee.

On a given day at your house, it seems that you have available to you every electronic device that has been invented in the last half century: microwave oven, digital bathroom scale, fax machine, cordless telephone, automatic icemaker, voice-mail hookup, camcorder . . .
You look around the house for half an hour trying to find a ball of twine. You don't have one.

At 17, if you had asked someone for a glass of water and they had told you that you could either drink some from the tap for free, or pay them money for some old water that someone claimed to have put in a bottle in France and then shipped across the ocean, where it had sat around a hot warehouse for a while, you would have been much too smart to fall for that. You would have been much too smart, at 17.

4

The James Bond Pleasures, and Other Truths of 50

At 50, after going through much of your life being unsure about most things, you finally understand that there are certain irrefutable truths, not open to debate. These truths are many and varied, and you can count on them as if they were engraved in granite:

The James Bond pleasures are all bad for you.

You grew up thinking that the rules of life taught to you in Ian Fleming's James Bond novels, and in the Bond movies, were something you could depend on. When Bond completed a perilous assignment, and his boss, M, wanted to reward him by sending him somewhere to recharge and celebrate, M's instructions were almost always a paraphrase of the same litany:

"Go down to a Caribbean island, 007. Lie in the sun all day long. Have a good steak every night. Drink those vodka martinis of yours. Cavort with all the beautiful women you can meet.''

Today, thirty years later, all of those are considered to be a recipe for a person's downfall. M could lose his job for telling an employee to do those things. But if we consider our realization of this to be a striking revelation, we should pause to understand that it's really not much different from the slogan on our parents' basement-rec-room wall, burned into the pinewood plaque they bought at a county fair: ''The only things I like are either illegal, immoral, or fattening.''

The wording of life's truths may change, but the truths themselves seem rather constant. And while we're on the subject of James Bond, here's another truth:

You are older than James Bond. You are much older than the James Bond of those novels and movies ever was.

The Wednesday Theory of Life defines everything.

The week always peaks with Wednesday; it did when you were a kid in school, and it has all during your adult working life. Monday and Tuesday are the reluctant and creaky start to the week, and on Wednesday you go over the hump—once Wednesday is done with you have a clear and unfettered view of the weekend ahead.

At 50, you come to the understanding that this applies to life, too. At a certain point in your life—and you sense you are now at that point—it's Wednesday. If your life has been some sort of constant climb, where in your head you're always applying for every job (both literal and figurative), hoping for every opening, striding ever up the mountain, now you're at Wednesday. You look down the other side of the mountain and you think you can see the weekend of your life waiting for you.

You hope this is not where they got the phrase "over the hill."

Meanwhile, behind you, on the up side of the incline, other, younger men and women are applying for the jobs, hoping for the plaudits, on their long way to their own Wednesdays.

Many of the things you liked best at 17, it turns out, are the things you like best now—the friends, the cheeseburgers, the songs. The concept of "growing into more sophisticated tastes," you learn, does not always hold true. Instead, more and more, you come around to knowing that your first tastes were your truest tastes.

I was visiting one of my oldest friends, one of the guys with whom I spent the most sun-washed and happy summers of my teenage years. He is an extremely wealthy man now; he lives in one of the most sumptuous and expensive houses in our old hometown. People approach him deferentially, asking him to contribute to philanthropic causes. He is a solid citizen.

I hadn't been in his house for more than two hours before we were trying to crawl under his motion detector. He has a valuable art collection, and the motion detector is set to trip an alarm if anyone comes into the rooms where the art is. We were on our bellies, attempting to slither into the rooms without making the alarm wail. Men deep into middle age, men who allegedly have better things to do—and we were convulsing with laughter as we heard the siren, turned it off, then tried to crawl beneath the invisible electronic beam again. His wife was looking at us with an amused, not altogether disapproving expression; I looked into my friend's face and I saw the laughter and the joy of 1964. For that one moment, it seemed that the security system in his house was unnecessary; for that one moment, all the security you would ever want was right there in that room.

Later we went out for a burger. All the pastry chefs in all the expensive restaurants in the world, and none of them can come up with anything that tastes better than a piece of banana cream pie with your first friends on those first nights of summer.

"They left this. It's yours."

I was staying in a hotel, and I heard one of the housekeepers say this to another housekeeper. Both were working for minimum wages. A family who had been on vacation had checked out the day before, and evidently had left an envelope containing a tip for the woman who had cleaned their room every day.

But that woman had taken a day off on the day the family checked out. The housekeeper who covered for her that day had found the envelope on top of the dresser. Now she was giving it to the other housekeeper—who would never have known about it were it not for her colleague's gesture.

I watched this, and I thought: The ethics and honor of this woman are so much higher than that of so many of the objectively successful business executives I have known in my life. The money was there when she went into the room; no one would ever have been the wiser if she were to keep it for herself. After all, it said "Maid" on the envelope. But it wasn't intended for her, and there was no way she was going to keep it. I thought of all the top-income corporate executives who stay in this hotel on company expense accounts (perhaps, in their hurry, not remembering to leave tips for the housekeepers)—and I thought about how those business leaders could do well to strive to become what the housekeeper with the envelope had become.

"They left this. It's yours." At 50, you realize that an

entire curriculum in business school could be built around those words.

Of all the difficult and exotic mysteries of life you have learned to unravel during your half century on Earth, the most complex and enduring of all may turn out to be parallel parking.

At 50, if you know one thing for sure, it is this:

Those hot dogs that are rotating on the metal rollers behind the glass? Don't buy them.

At some point during your lifetime, store names got cute.

The bakery called Let Them Eat Cake. The used-clothing store called Second Hand Rose. The store that sells socks called This Little Piggy. The maternity shop called A Pea in the Pod. The lingerie shop called I See London. The florist called This Bud's for You.

You are expected to put your faith in these stores precisely because they operate with a smile and a wink. The tacit message from the stores is: We're like you. We don't take ourselves too seriously. Life is a grin.

You think of the store names of your growing-up years. Taylor's Luggage. Ralph and Jim's Barber Shop. Connell's Flowers. Salt Brothers Hardware. Ross Cleaners.

You wonder whether Mr. Ross had a smile on his face when he opened the door to his laundry shop every morning. Whether Ralph and Jim saw life as endless mirth. At 50, you realize that the proprietor of the Add Water and Stir bathing suit store probably doesn't, either.

As much as you'd like to, you can't argue with facts:

More than 20 percent of all the presidents in the history

of the United States have been president during your lifetime.

"Adults Only" means the opposite.

The movies labeled "Adults Only" are usually filled with
imbecilic violence, crude sexuality, bathroom humor and
obscenity-saturated dialogue. No self-respecting adult
would want to identify himself or herself with the intellect
and values that are a part of these movies. Yet—understand-
ably—that is the label Hollywood is comfortable with. The
studios and producers would likely resist a change to the
more accurate "For Morons Only."

At 50, you think about what message children are receiv-
ing when they are told that the qualities people display in
these movies typify the way adults behave—that this is what
is waiting for those children when they reach adulthood.

Also a problem: the meaning of "For Mature Audiences."

The five-star hotels of the world, the celebrated gourmet
restaurants, the most elegant clothing . . .

Who are they for?

Certainly they are not for you. You think—when you
think about them at all—that you aren't ready for them yet.
But if you're not ready at 50, then when will you be ready?
And if these places and finery aren't intended for you, at
50, then who are they intended for?

It gradually dawns on you that many of the men and
women who are staying at those hotels, eating at those restaurants, wearing those garments, are considerably younger
than you are. You ask yourself how they managed to get old
enough to do this. While you are still waiting.

• • •

After all those years in school of staying up late, studying for midterms and finals, struggling to memorize all the information, you at last realize the truth:

On everything in life that matters, you are allowed to look it up before you give your answers.

Life is an open-book test.

Except, of course, for your memories.

"I feel *great!*"

It always catches you by surprise, when someone booms out that high-decibel response to the simple query of: "How are you?"

You're accustomed, at 50, to seeing any number of men and women who go through life grim and somber. Them, you can get a read on. But the ones who backslap and tell you jokes without prompting and beam maniacally at you— the "I feel *great!*" people—them, you don't know about.

You ask yourself whether the guy who looks so serious all the time really is. Because you know this: The other guy, the ceaselessly laughing guy, can't really be so carefree.

"Da Doo Ron Ron" holds the secret.

You finally figure out that one of the keys to rock and roll success is, and always has been, to sing the most utterly silly words with complete conviction—or, as a corollary, to express heartfelt pain in happy-sounding upbeat-tempo songs.

The Crystals sang "Da Doo Ron Ron" as if those words contained the most anguishing, universal truths in all of human history—and, because their voices played it straight, it worked. The Beatles sang deeply felt words of heartbreak and rejection—"I'm a Loser," "Help!"—and, because the songs were bright and bouncy, people swallowed them like medicine mixed with sugared syrup.

The Beatles wrote of feeling alone and empty, of having

no one to turn to—and they delivered the message in a cheerful way listeners could dance to. The marriage of the two, you realize at last, is what made it all work. Papa-Ooo-Mow-Mow . . .

You begin to think that full self-confidence never really kicks in. For anyone.

For my friends and me, when we were growing up, the funniest person alive was Jonathan Winters. He could read a grocery shopping list aloud and make us collapse into howls. We never met him—we saw him only in the movies or on television—but he represented, to us, the idea of comedy as genius, comedy as birthright.

One night in the 1980s I was supposed to be on David Letterman's old late-night show on NBC. The show was taped at 5:30 in the afternoon, at the same time that, across a hallway in Rockefeller Center, the local NBC station's early newscast was on the air live.

That day, Jonathan Winters—promoting one project or another—was a guest on the WNBC local newscast. Letterman apparently saw him on a monitor. When Winters came out of the WNBC studio, Letterman approached him and asked if he'd like to stick around and drop in on his network show.

Winters said no. I saw him say to Letterman and his producers that he didn't feel confident that he'd be good enough that night. "I don't have anything ready," Winters said. He had nothing prepared he thought would be sufficiently funny for the Letterman show.

Who would have guessed it? Jonathan Winters, unsure. But it is entirely logical. Whether you're a comedian or a sales representative, a labor negotiator or a schoolteacher, maybe, as full as confidence as you try constantly to appear, there's always a part of you that knows the confidence is a mask.

I walked past two women who appeared to be in their 60s. I heard one telling the other:

"The article said it's really bad for you."

I knew she was right. It didn't even matter what article she was referring to. The revised James Bond theory again. It's bad for you. That, you learn at 50, is something you can count on.

As a person who was raised on dictionaries, you're not sure why, but you think the spell-check function on personal computers may signal the end of learned civilization as we know it.

The fire goes out.

You can see it in certain people you've known for much of your adult life—especially those who are a little older than you. It seems to happen to them at some point after 50.

They're people you have worked with. The look in their faces, the way they move around the office, the sound of their voices, and, especially, the cast of their eyes—you can see that the fire is gone.

You don't know how it happens—whether it happens on a certain day, or gradually, over time. And you don't know whether it has to happen—whether it's inevitable if a person lives long enough.

You hope not. When the fire is burning it is something you never really notice, something you hardly know is there. Until the day you look at a person you've known for so long, and you see that the fire is doused.

• • •

There is no censor.

Maybe there never was, at least in the form of one person, but you assumed the censor was present. Certain things, people were not supposed to see—not just young people, but anyone. As children you heard vague tales about the "network censors," a phrase usually pronounced with vague disapproval, and if you never actually recall such a censor having a name, you knew he—the censor was presumed to be a he—was there.

Because of the unseen censor, the most graphic sex and violence, the most vivid and forbidden material, consisted of things you had never witnessed, but you knew existed. With all the pornography and carnage available today, delivered via satellite and cable to American homes, the most terrifying and ominous piece of television programming ever, still buried somewhere deep in the subconscious of many Americans now in middle age, was an episode of an old ABC series called *Bus Stop*. The name of the episode was "A Lion Walks Among Us."

It never aired in many parts of the country. Officials at many ABC affiliate stations decided it was too raw and disturbing for a television audience to see, and refused to broadcast it. The guest star of the episode was Fabian; his career, as I recall, was temporarily hurt because of his involvement with the program so many people never saw. Even today, the sound of that title—"A Lion Walks Among Us"—has the capacity to chill and titillate. By refusing to let the audiences see it, the censors who killed the show in their towns gave it a power—a haunting, continuing echo—that it would likely never have possessed otherwise.

"A Lion Walks Among Us," for people who are 50, may have been the last landmark of a society in which forbidden meant forbidden—in which forbidden was not a marketing slogan or something said with jaded sarcasm, but a pronouncement that someone really did exist who had the authority to forbid.

Parental guidance? The unseen censors seemed to realize that the parents could be idiotic. It wasn't just the children of America who were being kept away from certain material. It was America itself. Now, for better or for worse, the censor is dead. We're on our own.

"Could you do me a favor?"

It may be the most-spoken phrase in the offices and factories of the United States. "Could you do me a favor? Copy these reports for me?" "Could you do me a favor? Run this up to Accounting on the eighth floor?" "Could you do me a favor? See if these numbers are in line with what we projected last quarter?"

Actually, it's sort of a nice illusion. There are no favors involved. Everyone is there because they're being paid to be there. In an increasingly uncivil social structure, it may be the last remaining outpost of taken-for-granted politeness: "Will you do me a favor?" Meaning: "Do this."

Certain other phrases, when you are 50, take on new meaning. Some of them you don't want to think about too deeply.

Such as: "A secret he carried to his grave."

All of a sudden it's not just something out of old movies and mediocre novels. There are things that men and women know about themselves, about their families, that they will never tell anyone. Whatever the burdens of bearing those secrets are, for some people they no longer seem temporary. They've been borne long enough that the phrase about carrying them to the grave is no longer necessarily fanciful.

On a somewhat less depressing note about a somewhat

cheerier phrase: At 50 you finally figure out that "the hospitality room" isn't. They don't mean it—they're not being hospitable to you, and they aren't really doling out hospitality, and you shouldn't feel obliged to go there. If you move in more affluent circles—country clubs and polo outings—you can be confident that this applies to the hospitality tent, too.

The New Year's Eve Dictum is incontrovertible.

Which is: Nothing good happens when you try to plan it.

The reason New Year's Eves—you finally realize this, fifty years on—are always such a bust is that if you set up an occasion in advance with the idea that it is going to be great and memorable, it won't be. The only truly great things—the ones that last, the ones that stay with you forever—come when you aren't expecting them.

Whether it's waiting for a phone call or planning a celebration, you now know that the phone calls and celebrations that thrill and endure are the ones you didn't anticipate. Every experience, from first love on forward, tells us this is true.

So why, this far into our lives, knowing that the New Year's Eve Dictum cannot be questioned, do we try to ignore this knowledge? Why do we still try to plan the wonderful things?

It may be the definition of optimism—waiting for goodness, writing it on a calendar, not quite counting on it, but allowing the hope that if we set the table for it, it will arrive.

I was having dinner with a man about ten years older than I am; he was going through a bad period at his office.

He was talking about his boss—a man considerably younger—and he said:

"He doesn't like my work."

I thought it was not only an honest thing to say, but a brave one. It's a sentence we don't usually say—because, on some level, we are afraid that the boss may be right, or at least that the people we are telling about it will think he is.

When we say a sentence like that—"He doesn't like my work"—we are conceding that we have no say over our own lives: that what someone else thinks of us is, in certain ways that matter, arguably more important than what we think of ourselves.

My older friend said those words to me, and behind the words was the recognition that careers have ebbs and flows, that the younger men and women who come to the company after us and rise above us may think that all the men and women who have been our bosses before, men and women who valued our skills, have been wrong.

"He doesn't like my work," my friend said, sounding as if he were talking not about himself but about some other person. Which, in a way, he was.

If you're having trouble dealing with the concept of being 50, and you aren't sure why, it may be that somewhere inside you are aware of certain people who never got that old.

John F. Kennedy. Elvis Presley. John Lennon. All the things they accomplished, they got done before they became as old as you. They got it done and were gone.

Complex and heavily promoted, you realize at 50, does not always outshine elementary and humble.

Quadraphonic sound is dead and buried. The safety pin, on the other hand, will live forever.

One thing you know by now:

Anytime they show a carnival in a movie, something terrible is going to happen. Anytime a scene is set on the Fourth of July, you can count on a dark and sinister plot twist.

They can't fool you anymore. It's taken you half a century sitting in the audience to figure it out, but you know that when they show you lightness and joy, they're setting you up for a fall.

Something about menus, signboards, and office directories is somehow less impressive now that you know it's all done on a computer.

The old daily menus at downtown hotels—with the specials of the day crisply and elegantly printed—felt important and big. The idea of a printshop somewhere off the property, with someone setting type and proofreading it—it made you think you were a part of something larger than you. In its own minor way, it made the world seem expansive. Major.

At 50 you go through life seeing the signs, the leaflets, the menus, and you think of a kid running his cursor down the computer screen in his bedroom, choosing colors, choosing fonts. Anyone can do it. There's no mystery; a child can do it. Hit the "print" button.

What you were taught in physics was accurate, in ways that have nothing to do with numbers or charts:

One of the strongest forces in nature is inertia.

It has affected more lives and defined more human activity than just about anything else. Look at the life stories of the people you have known. That which stays put, tends to stay put. That which is put in motion moves and moves and moves.

You need something, and your first instinct is, "I'll call the department store and have it delivered."

It only takes you half a second to realize: Wait a minute. I don't go to department stores anymore. And I haven't seen a department store delivery truck on my street in thirty years.

You're at a party with friends in the summertime, and you think, but don't say: I really don't need to see anyone's 50-year-old feet in a pair of open-toed sandals.

You can't name any of the last twenty astronauts.
    The melancholy thing is that children can't, either.

It comes full circle.
    Just like when you were a kid, the people you admire and respect the most are firefighters.

5

Perspectives from Miles Off Youthquake Beach

At 50, as the news of the world, both momentous and minor, bombards you from every direction, you are finally able to take it all in with some sense of perspective:

You are at the point in your life at which cute stories about presidential cats and presidential dogs fail to amuse you. More to the point, you realize instantly what the strategy behind those stories is: a heavy-handed attempt by a White House staff to humanize the president—every president, president after president—with the public, and thus shift focus away from the job the president has been hired to do.

As soon as the television news begins to show a whimsical report about the president's wacky troubles with his cat or dog, you change to another channel. You don't even think your own dog is particularly cute. You're certainly not going to spend any time thinking about the president's dog.

• • •

Whenever you're going through certain doleful moments about being 50, you can always put it into perspective by reminding yourself:

Hey, Hugh Hefner is 70.

For some reason, this does not make you feel all that better.

This is probably because each issue of *Playboy* magazine, on the occasions you still see it these days, makes you feel once again like that decrepit and invisible person on Youthquake Beach.

The Playmate of the Month becomes somewhat less enticing when you look at her "biography" on the back of the centerfold, and see that she was born during a year when you were passed over for your first job promotion.

At 50, you now understand that some doctors, attorneys, accountants, and brokers finished in the bottom 20 percent of their classes.

And you have no way of knowing which ones they are.

I was in a restaurant waiting to meet some people for dinner. There were other men and women in the bar area, also waiting for their tables.

One of the men at the bar, an older fellow, had a rather unusual ring on one of his fingers. It was big, heavy—it had the look of a high school class ring.

But it wasn't. It was a 1956 World Series ring.

Someone asked him about it. He said that his name was Mickey McDermott, and that he had been a pitcher on the '56 New York Yankees.

"By '56, I was on my way out," he said.

He told the people at the bar about riding the trains

during the years before major-league baseball teams flew everywhere, about playing with Mickey Mantle and Yogi Berra and Whitey Ford, about the feeling of stepping onto the pitcher's mound in front of a full house in Yankee Stadium.

The people waiting for their tables weren't quite sure whether this man was putting them on. He mentioned the name of Walt Dropo—another big-league ballplayer of that era—who apparently was going to join him for dinner, but whose name didn't mean anything to the people who were listening to him. Mickey McDermott said that he was attempting to write an autobiography, which he said he had tentatively titled "A Funny Thing Happened on the Way to Cooperstown." He said his ghostwriter was "the former PR man for Eddie Fisher."

Later, I asked a friend who is in his 60s about McDermott. Sure, he said, he remembered McDermott: "In the 1940s there was a big full-page picture of him in *Life* magazine. The reason they put him in the magazine was that he had such a baby face for a major-league ballplayer—he was a pitcher for the Red Sox then, and he had this baby face."

I thought about the lesson of this. If you can be a pitcher for the New York Yankees—if you can be a part of the 1956 Yankees World Series championship team, one of the most glorious teams in history, if you can pitch in Yankee Stadium and smile off the pages of *Life* magazine, and, having done all that, if you, forty years later, have to explain to strangers who you are and what you have done . . .

If that's what it inevitably comes to even for Mickey Mc-Dermott of the New York Yankees, then the rest of us can probably take it for granted that it will happen to us, too. That no matter what we think we have accomplished in life, no matter how lasting we fool ourselves into thinking our successes and contributions are, the day will come when we will be sitting with a group of blank-faced younger strangers, struggling to explain who we are and what we have done during our time on the planet.

Like a job application handed to a personnel officer after we have stopped working, we will be laying out our résumés, hoping for a favorable reaction. And we won't have World Series rings to help us along.

It strikes you, with a jolt, that you now have nostalgic feelings about your adult life.

This sneaks up on you. Nostalgia has always been something you felt toward moments of your childhood, moments with your family and your high school friends. That was the definition of nostalgia—fond memories of the days when you were a kid, an unformed person growing up.

But now you encounter a flash of something from the 1970s—a movie, a song, a picture of a celebrity—and you get a wash of happy nostalgia, and it occurs to you that you've been an adult for so long now that nostalgia has been redefined. You can yearn for and be warmed by things that happened not when you were a kid, but when you were a man or woman. You can look back across the decades not toward the child you were—but toward the young adult you were, which sometimes feels just as distant.

Something that happened in 1971 or 1976 feels like it happened last Tuesday, and it also feels like it happened all this history ago. It telescopes—time past feels close and far away, all at once. A song by the Hollies comes on the radio, and you remember where you were when you heard it, a few years back—and then you realize that the time and place you are thinking of, the time and place when you heard the song, was twenty-five years ago. At 50, twenty-five years ago feels like a few years back.

• • •

And the corollary:

Jane Pauley is Barbara Walters.

The young public people of your young adult years have become—that bittersweet phrase—the seasoned veterans. Jane Pauley was the new Barbara Walters (back when that Hollies song was playing, back when she first went on the *Today* show), but now, to young broadcasters wanting to break in, she is not, as she is to us, the bright kid. She's Barbara Walters—she's been there forever, she's done everything, she has the Barbara Walters role.

Except that Barbara Walters is still Barbara Walters. If all of this is confusing for us, think of what it feels like for her.

This applies to your office, too. Just look around you.

Who won last year's Super Bowl?

Answer quickly.

Who won the World Series two years ago? The Masters last spring?

At 50, you understand with a smile that the things that are supposed to have such importance in the national life— the big games that America stops what it's doing to watch— are simply our modern-day opiate of the masses, a method to deliver bodies to advertisers. You can't easily come up with the name of the team that won the big game, because there have been so many big games that they all blend together. Like the Playmate of the Month, that power forward or linebacker you are asked to hold in such esteem was a baby in a bassinet when you were 28 years old and going to work every day, hoping for a raise. Before the linebacker knows it, he'll be in front of the TV set some Super Sunday, watching another linebacker who right at this minute is in another bassinet.

•   •   •

This putting-everything-in-perspective thing is not exactly foolproof, by the way.

For example, you can tell yourself that a quick way to determine the measure of a truly happy and fulfilling life is to ask if, had a certain person never been born, would the world have been graced by the beauty of his work? A painter's paintings would never have existed had this individual painter not been a part of the human race. But a partner in an accounting firm, regardless of how affluent and successful, still comes up with the same answer at the end of a column of figures as any other person adding those numbers up.

This theory of joy and personal satisfaction falls apart, however, when you see all the anguished and depressed painters in the world—and all the glowingly happy accounting-firm senior partners parring the fourteenth hole at the Tournament Players Club.

Whenever the world begins to seem too hemmed in and confining to you, you can play the "There's-a-sentence-that's-never-been-spoken-before" game.

It will fill you with renewed reverence for the infinite size and scope of our planet.

Every day, you will hear sentences that have never been spoken before, and will never be spoken again.

They're not momentous sentences:

"What Dr. Masser did for her was kind of like a helping hand."

"Jeff was wrong about the fuel pump over at the Montrose plant, because it's not functioning at all."

"Lisa says she needs a tutor, but if you ask me, three quiet hours a night up on that third floor of the library would do the trick."

You can stop and listen to what's being said around you,

and you can think: There are only twenty-six letters in the alphabet, yet in all of human history these words have never been spoken in this order before, and never will be again, to the end of time. It seems like a frivolous little exercise, yes—but it puts you, and all of us, in our place in the world.

Which is very small, just moving through.

"What are you talking about?"

The question came from a 6-year-old boy. I had been talking with his dad about the major-league baseball strike of 1994 and 1995. This boy, along with his 10-year-old brother, was a part of the conversation.

The father was saying he would never forgive the ballplayers and the owners for screwing up two seasons. The 10-year-old, too, was angry at baseball: "They're all jerks," he said.

But the 6-year-old—"What are you talking about?"—didn't remember. He was young enough that, for him, it was history that didn't exist. His memory of such things hadn't kicked in yet.

Which, at 50, is sort of a pleasant thing to keep in mind. The things that seem so pressing and essential to any of us at a given moment will, eventually, be just a dim rumor to those who will later come along. "What are you talking about?" Oh, World War I. The Beach Boys. The Dark Ages.

Before your time.

One of the most tranquil phrases there could ever be.

The wake-up calls of a lifetime, and the thoughts, at 50, of what they were all for:

When you're a kid, you don't even think of needing an alarm clock. What for? You'll wake up when you wake up.

When you're old enough to go to school, you resent the alarm clock every time it rings.

As a young person out of college, with your first job that sends you on the road, you feel vaguely important leaving a wake-up call with the hotel's front desk—you're a part of the world of business travelers, all of you needing to be promptly awakened for the appointments ahead.

At 50, you go into a fury if the wake-up call you have left doesn't ring on schedule. How could they? How *could* they? You specifically left the call for 7 A.M., and they forgot to do it. Never mind that you're already awake at 7 A.M. (you're always awake at 7 A.M.). That's not the point. What if you'd overslept (you never oversleep; you seldom sleep at all)? How could they have forgotten?

Soon enough, you will circle around to the point at which you don't want or need any wake-up calls, any alarms. What for? What's so important that you have to wake up at a certain time of the morning?

Like the kid you used to be, you'll wake up when you wake up.

The free-and-clear question:

You ask yourself who, among all of us, is free and clear? If that's the goal—to achieve everything a person could achieve, to have no more questions about yourself, to be as secure and placid about your life and your accomplishments as a person can possibly be—then who among us has that feeling? Who, after all the striving, is free and clear?

There used to be an easy answer: the president of the United States. The president, among all of his contemporaries, has triumphed; the president has prevailed.

At 50 you think of the president's life, and you realize that he may be less free and clear than anyone. And that if free and clear is the finish line—the line we're all trying to cross—then maybe no one ever really reaches it.

• • •

The American Movie Classics channel—that terrific, com-
mercial-free cable channel featuring continuous black-and-
white movies from the 1930s, '40s, and '50s—is such a success not only because the movies are good, but because they
allow us a look at our country's social history.

It's the stuff you don't find in textbooks—what the streets
and houses looked like, how people talked, how they
treated each other, what the stores and restaurants felt like.
Yes, it's a Hollywood version—but it's also like a series of
snapshots, a scrapbook of what the world was like before all
of us grew to take charge.

And it gives you pause to think: What will future generations think of our world—the world we're living in right
now—when they watch some American Movie Classics offshoot in the distant future? When today's movies represent
the good old days?

The violence, the obscenity, the meanness, the casual in-
civility, the explosions, the carnage—what will they think
about the times in which we lived?

And will they be right?

On a cross-country flight on a cloudless day you can look
out the window of the plane and down at the hundreds of
cities you pass over, and think:

All the time, all the money, all the ambition and energy
and lifetimes spent so that people can be a few blocks closer
to the part of town where the trees and water are, a few
blocks farther away from the railroad tracks and factories.
The airplane in which you ride is over the town and on to
the next in a matter of seconds.

You can look around you in the plane and think: all the
time, all the money, all the ambition spent so that some of
these passengers can sit a few feet closer to the front, past
the curtains, in seats that are a few inches wider. Down

below there is already another new city—where even now, residents strive endlessly to be a few blocks better off.

Here's something that, at 50, has the potential to drive you crazy:

If, during the 1968 Democratic National Convention—the first convention that was a huge and gaudy story to you—you remember having read references to the tumultuous old-time Democratic convention of 1948, the Harry Truman convention . . .

Then that means that to young people right now, if they look back on politics over the same perspective of twenty years, their hazy, dusty-museum-wing political figures are Jimmy Carter and Ronald Reagan and Gerald Ford. Those are their faded tintypes, their antique political forefathers.

If, when you were a kid in 1956, in awe of the Yankees (the Yankees of Mickey Mantle and, yes, Mickey McDermott), and you knew even back then that the classic old-time baseball team was the '27 Yankees, the Yankees of Ruth and Gehrig . . .

That means that to young people right now, if they look back on sports figures over the same perspective of twenty-nine years, their ancient and distant athletic icons are Joe Namath and Earl Monroe and Johnny Bench and Lee Trevino. Those are the dusty names from the creaky and far-distant past. You can do this to yourself using any field of endeavor as the landmark—you can figure out what was old-time to you, and then calculate what is old-time to today's young men and women. But you probably shouldn't. Because if you do, you will understand the true meaning of the phrase:

"You're history."

• • •

Another phrase, one you hear every day:
"That's unbelievable!"
It's used to describe news events, sports highlights, developments in the personal lives of people you know, promotions and demotions at the office.
"Unbelievable!"
"That is *unbelievable.*"
"Un-be-*lievable*!"
At 50, you have come to know something:
Everything is believable. There is nothing that is unbelievable.
It is, at the same time, the most meaningless and most overused word in our national lexicon.
"Unbelievable!"
No it isn't.
Believe it.

Perspective, if it means anything, expands incrementally with age.
When you're 50, you look back with a certain wistfulness at an America that was prosperous and strong and the envy of the world. That America—the bustling, booming, Main-Street-solid America of the late 1940s, the 1950s, and the early 1960s—is, to the generation that is now 50, the remembered America past, the America worth recapturing.
But, of course, to our parents' generation, that is not their first American memory. They grew up during the Depression, in days when it sometimes seemed the country would never rise again. They recollect something that we can only read about—an America rocked back on its heels, an America that seemed lost, an America out of money and almost out of time.
So how odd it must seem for them—the generation of our mothers and fathers—to know that we regard the

steady, abundant, confident America of the 1950s as the dominant past. And how amazing it must have been for them to live through that reversal—to live in an America awash in unending national poverty, and so soon after to live in an America of two-car garages and suburban porches and sound, stable banks on every city corner. To see that sunny way of life accepted as a given, so soon after the terrible American days.

Their perspective is richer than ours. They have lived long enough to learn from the cycles of life, and of history, in a way that we, even at 50, have not. They know that a country can go from darkness to light with a relative swiftness that all but defies comprehension.

And, because they know that, they also sense how quickly it all can cycle back. Their optimism is ever tempered.

Speaking of their generation:

"Do you remember that!"

I heard those words at a fiftieth-anniversary party for a man and woman in their 70s. There had been a picnic that had concluded thirty minutes before; someone had videotaped it, had popped the cassette into the machine inside the house, and now everyone was watching the picnic that had just ended.

"Do you remember that!" someone called out happily, pointing at the television screen, referring to something amusing that had happened at the picnic.

Well . . . yes. Yes, we all remembered that. It had happened within the hour.

Another permutation of the one-hour-photo-stores phenomenon, this one even more skewed: Calling back fond memories, through videotape, that have happened in the hours since the sun last rose. Replaying history that is not history yet. Altering the meaning of history, and of memories.

I looked at the people whose anniversary it was. They were looking at themselves on the television screen, obligingly remembering themselves as they had been at the picnic. Outside the house, the picnic table had not yet been cleared.

And the most indelible memories, you know at 50, do not necessarily appear on a screen.

When I was a boy, there appeared one Saturday afternoon at the Lazarus department store downtown two singers promoting their new records. One was Tommy Edwards, whose song was "It's All in the Game"; one was Dale Hawkins, whose song was "La-Do-Dada." They weren't actually singing—they stood on a little stage near the record department, and someone put their songs on a record player and they lip-synched.

This was in the days when you could take a record into a listening booth, play it to see if you liked it, and then decide whether to spend the forty-nine cents for the 45 rpm single. About sixty or seventy of us boys and girls had come to the store, and we watched Tommy Edwards, a young black crooner, move his mouth to "It's All in the Game," and then we watched Dale Hawkins, a young white sneerer, sing "La-Do-Dada," and most of us bought copies of their records. It was hand-to-hand selling at its most elemental; they had come to central Ohio just to do this, to sell a few records.

Tommy Edwards must have hopped right on a train or a plane after the Lazarus show, because the next night he was on *The Ed Sullivan Show*. I remember watching that show with my parents and my sister and brother, and how distant Tommy Edwards seemed—how less real than the man I'd seen thirty hours before in the Lazarus record department. The *Ed Sullivan* appearance is vague and lost in time to me now, but I can still see Tommy Edwards on that little stage at Lazarus, his lips moving to the record that was spinning on the machine plugged into the department store wall. I can still feel what it was like to stand there, a kid, watching and listening. Hand-to-hand selling, then as now, is still the most effective. And memories that are never televised are still the most enduring.

When you are young, all airline pilots, even the ones in their 20s and 30s, seem old and in control. You're happy with them flying the plane.

Then, when you get a little older yourself, the pilots, even the ones in their 40s and 50s, don't seem so old after all. You wish the airlines didn't have that 60-and-out rule—you'd be just as happy with some of those gray-haired, retired military fellows at the controls forever.

Now, as you pass 50 and move in the direction of 60 yourself, you have decided that you can live with the 60-and-out rule. Because, you think, that's going to be you before too long. And you certainly wouldn't want you flying the plane.

Each December, when you read those year-end news wrap-ups in the paper, you become more and more convinced that the stories that make headlines, the stories that dominate the news broadcasts in a given year, will in the end have little effect on the real history of your life—the history that matters to you.

The news isn't. The details may change, but the news is un-new. There is nothing revelatory about it; the news, in its own way—the crimes, the floods, the earthquakes, the political upheavals—is as predictable as the seasons. Just fill in the different names and dates and locales.

The news in your life, you now know, is written beneath the roof of your house, inside the walls of the place where you go to work. It is heard only in your heart. All of the old truths, over all the centuries of mankind—all of the old truths seem suddenly new.

I was talking with a young baseball player named Chris Snopek. He was 25; he was just on the verge of making it to the majors full-time. At 25 he was a man who had accomplished that, which is saying something. A major-leaguer. Someone to look up to.

Even when you're 50. He was a very pleasant fellow, and as we talked, one adult to another, I thought silently that in the year that he was born, I was the age that he is now—and that the second twenty-five years of your life go by much faster than the first.

And the third twenty-five? Probably best not to think about that.

One of those things you know for a fact at 50:

Regardless of how many stories in how many national publications say that a new kind of comic books—literately written, artfully drawn—is becoming accepted reading for adults, you know that's wrong.

Comic books were something you read in the barbershop when you were 8. *Archie, Sad Sack, Superman, Men at War*—they were wonderful. You looked forward to each crisp and brightly colored new edition; even the outdated, faded issues, their pages flipped through so many times that they felt like tissue paper, issues you'd read a dozen or more times, continued to please you.

You are 50 years old. You don't care what anyone tells you—you aren't reading any more comic books.

Every day of your life you have tried, at least in some way, to do your best. It's been a basic tenet of how you have lived.

So why, at 50, if you consider the prospect of making a list of all the things you wish you could have done a little better—or a lot better . . .

Why, when you think of that mythical list, do you know beyond any possible doubt that the list, were you to commit it to paper, would go on and on, a list to stretch beyond the farthest horizon?

6

Dana Andrews' Sons, Barbara Stanwyck's Daughters

Men and women; women and men. You'd think, by 50, you finally had it all figured out. You'd think that, but you would be wrong.

Walking determinedly along jogging paths every morning are the 50-year-old women in their black low-cut boxing-style shoes, the kind of shoes Floyd Patterson used to wear into the ring. The message seems to be: Inside I'm madder than you'd think and inside I'm tougher than I look. In my head I'm fighting for the welterweight championship of the world in the Polo Grounds.

Not that men are any better off.

A generation of males who grew up thinking that once they became men it was their duty to look like Glenn Ford or William Holden now must deal with the reality that the

ideal of virility wears a ponytail, earrings and a silver brace-
let. That's not only what virile looks like now—that's what
blue-collar looks like now. The 50-year-old man, confused,
sends his suits out to the cleaners, and worries because it's
been two weeks since he's had a haircut.

Near a swimming pool, I heard two women, each around
50, talking in the sun as one read a women's-interest magazine.

"Here's a good article," the first woman said, reading
aloud from the table of contents. " 'The Way to Snap Out
of Your Cycle of Anger.' "

She said it with a lilt in her voice, a sense of fun. She read
the title aloud with pleased excitement, the way her mother
might have read aloud a magazine article titled "Twenty
Uses for Old Kleenex Boxes."

Two men, same day as the women with the cycle-of-anger
article:

The men were walking along together. The first man
said:

"On the other hand, lenders are becoming much more
cautious . . ."

Not, at 50, like the women in their lives. But then, not
exactly like when they were boys, either.

Might as well be direct about it:

Women at 50 often have this unspoken thought about
the men in all of their lives:

*Gee, isn't it weird that we once actually thought they were attrac-
tive?*

Like their amused assessment of a speculative investment
suddenly gone sour. *Not only did we find them attractive—we
wanted to spend our entire lives with them!*

The sentiments are never expressed in just that way. But when women, at 50, get together, it can recurrently be heard just beneath the surface of every word.

"Four tickets, please."

My friend Jack Roth, lowering his voice about eight octaves, said those words to the bored man at the box office of the Parsons Art Theater in a run-down area of our hometown in 1962. We were 15; Jack looked older than the rest of us, so three of us waited around the corner as he tried to buy tickets to the dirty movie.

He failed. You had to be 21 to get into the Parsons, and it wasn't too hard a call for the man at the box-office window to make: If you see one 15-year-old kid standing by himself, trying to make his voice sound like Richard Basehart's, ordering not one but four tickets, you turn him away.

So we never got in. If we had, we probably would have witnessed an out-of-focus black-and-white film featuring women running around in their bras and underpants, most likely drinking highballs and smoking cigarettes. In 1962, that's about as dirty as even the dirty movies got.

If a person of any age wanted to seek out smutty stuff in 1962, he'd have to go look for it. He could go to a burlesque house, or set up a home-movie projector and watch a World War II–era stag film that someone's uncle's cousin had stashed away in a drawer. It was inaccessible, hard to find, usually not worth the trouble. Sex, as a commodity, was, like sex itself, a mystery.

Around 1993, as I walked down hotel hallways on the way to my room during business trips, I began to notice loud moaning and panting, punctuated by explicit sexual talk, coming from some of the other rooms. This was happening all the time. It seemed odd—if the business travelers were as worn-out, weary, and distracted as they usually looked at the check-in desks and in the elevators, they sure were find-ing the renewed energy to have a lot of sex in their rooms.

But they weren't. They were watching the dirty movies on the pay channels—that's what I was hearing in the hotel hallways. I—still, nearing 50, the guy waiting for Jack Roth to buy the tickets at the Parsons Art Theater—had always assumed that the "adult" movies—that phrase again—on the pay channels were fairly tame: go-go dancers in fringed tops, like on the old *Hullabaloo* TV show.

Boy, was I wrong. The movies available in the Hiltons and Hyatts and Sheratons of the world are as raw and explicit as pornography can possibly be. And it's all delivered very cleanly: A guest touches the right button on the remote control, the movie comes onto the screen, the hotel and the pay-movie distributor each make a little money, and when the guest checks out the notation on his bill is "1 in-room movie"—to the auditor going over his expense re-port back at the office, it could be *Mrs. Doubtfire.*

For a kid at home, the same kinds of movies, in only slightly milder forms, are available on HBO and Showtime. If kids wait up late enough at night, they can see all the sex and nudity they want. No travel, no disapproving man at the box office, instant delivery into a kid's quiet suburban bedroom. The distance and the mystery are gone, and once that happens, there's no going back. "Four tickets, please," Jack said, a 15-year-old tenor trying his best to sound like a baritone. Somehow it seemed more exciting when it was harder to find.

I heard a woman of 50 saying this to her daughter, a woman in her early 20s:

"The real reason their marriage is a success is that nei-ther of them worked on it as hard in their first marriages, and this time it's better for them because they're working on it."

As if marriage is a college course; as if it's a course that can be studied for, and if you get an incomplete the first semester you can take the course again and get an A the next term.

And maybe the mother was right. Yet as I looked at the two women—the daughter, whose expression as she listened to her mother talk hinted that she, for one, still wanted to view marriage as a place of romance and idealism and spontaneity, and her mother, who spoke of the potential pitfalls of marriage as she would speak about repairing an auto engine—I thought that, even if the mother was right, the daughter's way of thinking was better.

And I wondered how many years it would take before the daughter turned into the mother.

An addendum to the porno-in-the-Hyatts conundrum:

The aerobics-and-exercise shows on the cable sports channels—the *wholesome* stuff—are racier than anything they showed in the art theaters of 1962. If Jack had been able to get us those four tickets, and we had gone into the Parsons and seen one of those ESPN exercise shows from the shores of Hawaii, our eyes would have turned into pinwheels and we wouldn't have been able to walk straight for days.

What the generation of American men who are now 50 missed out on was the Dana Andrews model of manhood.

Dana Andrews isn't the movie star who comes to most people's minds when they think of his generation of stars— Gary Cooper and Clark Gable and Humphrey Bogart are the ones who remain legends. But Andrews, as a cinematic representation of how men used to see themselves, probably offers a clearer picture of the difference between our fathers' generation and ours.

He was buttoned-up and serious and responsible even in early adulthood. In *The Best Years of Our Lives*—as a young veteran coming home from World War II—he was a solid citizen, a person who would be pleased to be mistaken for a man ten years his senior. And he did, indeed, seem much older than his chronological age.

That, for some reason, is precisely the cinematic model that the generation of men now 50 rejected. If Dana Andrews and *The Best Years of Our Lives* represented young American manhood for our fathers' generation, then Peter Fonda and *Easy Rider,* Dustin Hoffman and *The Graduate,* represented it for ours. Perhaps it was no coincidence; perhaps we were consciously rejecting Dana Andrews' world— our fathers' world—by our choice of movies and movie stars. Dana Andrews as a young American man was ready to settle down. Maybe that's what we were running from.

Although if when we were young we missed out on the stone-faced, analytical, nose-to-the-icy-grindstone models of young American manhood, we don't have to go too far to find those models today.

They're our new young bosses—the young men (and women) at the office who are suddenly our supervisors, Dana Andrews reborn.

You have friends who, at 50, are at the very top of their fields—powerful, accomplished people who have in their lifetimes achieved very difficult and impressive things.

Then they get divorced—and you see they are made nervous and awkward over the prospect of asking someone to go out. They lose sleep over it. They rehearse it. They hesitate before picking up the phone to make the call.

It's not like riding a bicycle, they learn. You can't jump right back on and pick up where you left off.

Although, once they do get the hang of it again, the mating ritual of men and women at 50 can take on a somewhat sardonic tone.

They know the odds aren't with them. They've been through too many years of personal history, they've seen all the ways that men and women can fail in the pursuit of loving each other. They feel, at times, that they know too much.

So the attitude of men and women at 50—never uttered, always felt—is often: "All right, I dare you. I dare you to like me. I'm 50 years old with fifty years of flaws and wear, and here I am. I dare you. Come on. Match you and raise you one."

And if you think it's a different world at 50, look ahead to 70 and 80.

The good news is that, even at those ages, people flirt. It's not over yet.

You can see it in a quick exchange in a restaurant:

A woman in her 70s is looking for the restroom. When she gets there, it is one of those restrooms that don't have "Ladies" or "Women's" written on the door. Instead, it has a brass figurine of a stylized Grecian-era woman.

A man in his 70s, walking toward the men's restroom, passes her as she's looking at the door. It's apparent that she knows the man, but she is not his dinner partner for the evening.

"How do I know this is for women?" she says, smiling and gesturing toward the brass figure on the door. "Maybe it's for men who want to look at women."

He laughs lightly; she laughs lightly. To an outsider it may seem—awful, patronizing word—cute.

But to the woman and the man it's just another step in that long path that began in junior high school—the tentative "hi's" in the hallways, the decisions about whether to smile at a person you want to know better, the worries about what the other person may think of you, if the other person thinks of you at all. The long path along which every inflection of the word "hello," every variation of the way you say it, sends a message to the person on the other end.

It never stops—or at least it never has to. "Good morning," the man in his 80s says on his daily walk around his neighborhood. "It's a beautiful day," the woman in her 80s, walking the other way on the same sidewalk, says in return. They each proceed in their own direction, thinking their thoughts.

At 50, men still get a little ticked off when an invitation arrives and they see that it carries the notation: "Formal. Black Tie."

At 50, women still see the same invitation and think: "Oh, good. Formal. Black tie."

Two women at 50, evidently sharing a mordacious sense of humor and of the world's ridiculous ways, in midconversation:

"Someone once invented nail polish."

"I know. And we actually bought it."

Among the occasionally maddening aspects of being a woman at 50:

Being condescended to by women of 25 or 26 in the workforce who seem to feel that because a woman is 50, it needs to be explained to her carefully and slowly how things work these days in the world of business—as if the younger women see women of 50 as presuffragettes with bloomers, parasols, and rouge.

But who could possibly blame women of 50 for being a little chagrined at having to deal with the classic American movie stereotype of what happens as a woman grows older? Have you ever paid attention to the screen careers of Joan Crawford and Barbara Stanwyck? From glowing and radiant roles at 20 to scowling and bitter roles at 50?

Meanwhile, aging men got to be Cary Grant.

And the thought that women of 50 sometimes worry about a little in the middle of the night:

They are closer to their friends than they are to their husbands. Lunch with their friends is more satisfying than dinner with their husbands.

They're not sure whether to ask their mothers whether they ever felt the same way. They're afraid that by asking the question, they will be revealing to their mothers an answer.

Women know certain things at 50 that are completely lost on men.

A woman friend who was on a business trip told me that her hotel room was directly across from where the elevator door opened. Every time she would get off the elevator when men were also on board, she would walk down the hallway as if she were going to another room. Then, when the elevator door closed, she would walk back to her room and let herself in.

"A woman never wants her room to be right across from the elevator," she said. "It lets the men on the elevator know exactly where she is staying."

I had never heard this before.

"It's a problem men don't have," she said.

There are other things men don't think about, either. Such as this sentence, spoken with genuine interest by a woman of around 50 as she walked into the home of another woman of the same age:

"I've got a chair just like that. Machine-washable fabric, right? Double length, right?"

Undoubtedly an accurate observation. And a sentence few 50-year-old men would ever find themselves speaking.

Men and women who are 50 grew up hearing some among their more liberal-minded contemporaries say, "Nudity is beautiful. There's nothing wrong with nudity. The body is a beautiful thing."

Now they can honestly answer: Well, not really.

And in that area: In the summertime, it's got to be harder for women than for men. Because women who are 50 have gone from an America where the assumption about a bathing suit for females of any age was that it was one piece and baggy with a ruffled skirt starting at the waistline, to an America where the standard pool attire for women of any age is like something out of a striptease emporium—two bands of cloth, the bottom cut high on the hip and low on the belly, the kind of swimsuit that a person might be arrested for wearing in 1955.

Meanwhile, men at 50 get to wear the same droopy trunks that their fathers did. The unequal playing field of Cary Grant and Joan Crawford again.

Sometimes, when you are asking yourself whether there is still a genuinely satisfied wife anywhere in America, you stop to consider: There are millions upon millions of husbands who truly are satisfied.

This has to do with differing expectations. There are
women of 50 who look at their kitchens, and all they can
see is all the meals they've made, all the dishes they've
washed, thousands of meals and thousands of dishes over
dozens of years, for families that took the meals for granted
and hurried on to whatever they had planned next. There
are women who lie awake next to their husbands in bed at
night and wonder how they got here.

The husbands who are snoring next to them, on the
other hand, are often blissfully satisfied. They come home,
have dinner, and fall asleep. What's not to be satisfied
about?

I actually saw a young businessman—a guy in his early 30s—
on a pay phone making an appointment with his wife to
have phone sex.

He was at a trade convention out of town; he was asking
his wife when the children were going to bed, and checking
his company itinerary for the evening. He was one of those
earnest young fellows who look as if they are on the way up
through the corporate hierarchy.

He was looking at his watch to make sure he wasn't late
for his next business function, and at the same time using
some gooey words to describe to his wife what they were
going to do on the phone later. He was talking quite audibly. At pay phones on either side of him were older men,
men in their 50s, who looked at him as if to say: What, are
you *nuts*?

Of all the factors that have had a part in shaping women of
50 into who they are, the "girls don't call boys" dictum of
their growing-up years may rank at the top.

Girls believed it; boys believed it. In ways that went far beyond the original meaning of girls don't ask boys to go on dates, the girls-don't-call-boys axiom was a subtle but powerful determinant of who girls were taught to think they were, and what they were taught to think about life—and how the world changed while they were living in it.

They were the girls who were told that ladies' choice was an anomaly, a once-in-a-great-while occasion. Now those girls are 50, living in a world told to embrace the idea that ladies' choice is a way of life. And they all remember when it was not necessarily so.

Not to mention being members of the "Nothin' says lovin' like something from the oven" generation.

The most puzzling part of it for them is that often they feel it happens to be true. It's just something they wouldn't want to say out loud.

For men and women at 50 who are thinking about getting married again, all of the other questions inherent in the decision are joined by this one:

When you're 50, how do you deal with meeting the in-laws?

It was awkward enough at 22, when your prospective in-laws were 50. Today, they're 74, 76, 80. You're supposed to get to know them, tell them your life story, learn and remember theirs. Memorize the names of all the relatives.

"Honey, I'd like you to meet my parents."

It's such an exhausting concept, it makes you just want to go out for a long walk.

Why do women, at 50, stock up on books about how men don't understand them at all?

Not that it's not true. But why do they feel the need to see it written down on paper?

On the subject of "trophy wives," the beautiful young women whom wealthy and successful businessmen sometimes marry after a divorce:

When women of 50 see a man of 50 with his trophy wife, it's not so much that they resent what the man has done (although they do). More than that, though, it's that they look at the 24-year-old woman and feel like asking her, "Are you out of your *mind*? Are you seeing something different from what we see? *Look* at that guy. Are you *berserk*?"

Women, for the first time at 50, look at the new fall fashions and think: "Who are they *making* these for?"

Generalizations are seldom accurate. But the ultimate answer to why women at 50 are different from men at 50 can probably be found if someone ever figures out why, by a seashore, it's almost always the women who are collecting shells.

No more carpools.

For a woman at 50, that one phrase is drenched with both the promise of freedom, and the emptiness of something precious beyond words coming to an end. Something that was at the same time the best and the most confining thing in the woman's life. No more carpools. Maybe that, in a way, does have something to do with the shells she picks up so carefully, to take home and to save.

A man who knows he is loved, as evidenced in three short sentences spoken to his wife:

"You know what hurts?" the husband says. "The rest of my body's fine. What hurts is my elbows and my fingers."

She understands.

"I'm embarrassed to admit this," said the woman, at 50. "But there are times when I think about whether my egg salad is as good as my mother's. Don't laugh."

No one does.

All those phrases in the wedding vows? The boilerplate stuff—for better or for worse, for richer or for poorer, in sickness and in health?

It turns out that it means something. It's not the fine print.

All of those things can and do happen in the lifetime of a man or a woman—in the lifetime of a man and a woman.

When you were 22, they seemed like cobwebbed shibboleths from an antique and archaic old ceremony.

By 50 you realize that it was a contract. And you measure yourself by how faithfully you have honored it.

There is a lyric from a country song:

My heart's not ready for the rocking chair . . .

Which may be as hopeful a combination of words as you'll come across. After everything, we all still yearn.

7

The Saturday Night Crowd and Our Parents' America

The more you think of how your life has changed at 50, the more you understand that the essential differences often mirror the differences between your parents' world and yours. There are days when this hits you everywhere you look, in every way you can feel:

I once knew a homicide detective by the name of Joe DiLeonardi. He had seen human beings at their most depraved; he had been called to murder scenes that would haunt most people forever. Yet he managed to maintain.

Once I asked him how he retained his own humanity.

"When I was growing up," he said, "there was warmth and compassion in the house. There was laughter, too, but there was a sense of discipline. Even when I was in the service, when I'd be out on a pass at four in the morning, I could hear my mother's voice saying, 'Joe, get home.' And I'd go back to the barracks.''

At 50, sometimes that voice is all you have. Because there are nights when you ask yourself whether anyone is waiting up for you. Whether there is anyone thinking that you might be out too late, worrying that you're not home yet. You have to depend on that voice in your head. It is as important to you in distant echo as it was when the voice was really there.

My parents used to be a part of something that they called the Saturday night crowd.

It was a group of friends—young couples, all of them World War II veterans and their wives—who, each Saturday night, would gather at the home of one couple or another and have a party. I remember coming down the stairs to see all of them, drinking cocktails, smoking cigarettes (that was a part of the Saturday night crowd hosting routine—providing cigarettes, tip-up in silver-colored cups, for the gang), being loud and happy. In the home movies that I have looked at since, the men in the Saturday night crowd were all wearing suits and ties, the women were all wearing pretty dresses.

It's something that many of us, at 50, missed out on in our own adulthood. We may have had *Saturday Night Live* to link us, but the Saturday night crowd of our parents' generation—the weekly traveling party in our little town—never quite happened.

I envy them for having had it. Their own Saturday night crowd is no more—it ended by the time most of us, their children, had reached high school age. And our Saturday night crowd—the one that never was—somehow feels that it has faded away, too, without ever having raised a single toast.

· · ·

The singers we grew up listening to are finding it a little more awkward to turn 50 than did the singers our parents listened to.

When Frank Sinatra turned 50, for instance, it was in a tuxedo of the kind he had been wearing for years, and with a commemorative album called *A Man and His Music,* Nelson Riddle, Gordon Jenkins, Count Basie, Johnny Mandel and others conducting. Sinatra might as well have been a charter member of the Saturday night crowd—at 50 he had been a martinis-and-wisecracks guy for most of his life. For him 50 was a laudable goal that had inevitably been reached, something that felt comfortable and right.

For the Rolling Stones and the Who and the other bands whose music spoke to us the way Sinatra's spoke to our parents, 50 came around wearing white tights and spangled jackets and plugged into bulky black amplifiers. The music still moved us, but it felt vaguely wrong to have to sit in a football stadium to listen to it. Even the singers who have always had the steadiest sense of themselves realize the dilemmas of a rock and roller's life at 50; Bob Seger told me, "I meet people all the time who come up and say, 'My mom loves you.' Occasionally they'll say, 'My grandma loves you.' "

For a singer, 50 seems to have been easier to deal with when 50 wore that tux and clutched that highball under the stage lights. Back when the singer, at 50, could sing smoothly (to the alumni of the Saturday night crowd), "The most beautiful girl in the world, eats my candy, drinks my brandy . . ."

And mean it.

A number of new, planned communities are doing away with sidewalks.

The reason is that sidewalks—according to the community planners—are an invitation for strangers to walk by your house. Today's Americans, with their heightened sense of the need for security, want few things less than the prospect of seeing someone they don't know in front of their homes. People who live in those homes drive most places in their cars, anyway.

So the sidewalks are going. And when you think of the neighborhood where you grew up, with the sidewalks running in front of every house, the sidewalks serving as the connective threads of your community . . .

When you think of the sidewalks going away, you realize that as they disappear, so does a part of the expectation your parents gave you of what life is supposed to feel like.

David Eisenhower once told me a story:

"When I was 16, my grandfather sold me a '62 Plymouth Valiant that he had owned.

"He sold it to me for fifty dollars. The one rule I had to obey was that I would never exceed fifty-five miles per hour. I had to promise him that.

"I would drive my grandfather around Gettysburg, and the whole time I was driving he would keep his eyes on the speedometer, like a hawk. He didn't know if I had proper road judgment. When I was in college I got a speeding ticket, and it made the newspapers, and my family had to keep the newspapers away from my grandfather."

Now David Eisenhower is about to be 50, and Ike is long dead. David's burden may have been greater than those of most of his young contemporaries—the burden of pleasing Ike—but it is worth considering as we prepare to assume our own Ike-in-the-passenger-seat roles. Sitting there like a hawk, passing judgment on someone else's road skills, knowing in our hearts now as we knew in our hearts then that we will never be Ike. But, then, our fathers knew it, too. They might have hoped to achieve a lot of things in their lives. But they would never be Ike.

And their war—the war of our fathers' and mothers' generation—was also, in ways of which we are only gradually becoming fully aware, our defining war.

Contemporary sociology tells us that Vietnam was the defining war—even the defining event—of the generation of men and women now turning 50. Certainly it would be impossible to overestimate the effects of Vietnam upon the national heart.

Yet World War II, and what it did in forming our parents, turning them from the young people they were into the adults they became, may reside in our dreams in a way even more compelling than does Vietnam. For anytime men and women of 50 get that too-familiar sensation that they will never feel quite as solid as they remember their parents being, every time those men and women begin to sense a lack of stability, a vacuum where the steady center should be (that vacuum visible to no one else, a vacuum that is felt but never seen) . . .

Every time that happens, it seems to harken back to the ripples of World War II, and what the war made of our parents. We have known for a long time that so many men and women of the World War II generation consider the war to be the central circumstance of their lifetimes. What is becoming clear only now is that, in delicate and mysterious ways, it is also the central circumstance of their children's lifetimes.

Brought into sharp contrast as the World War II generation leaves us, and we realize anew that they were our definition of what we ought to become—and that, in many and continuing ways, we fear that we have not.

• • •

What we missed, and what our parents had, was 1951.

We were too young in 1951 to know just what that year meant. And our parents couldn't have known, either—1951 undoubtedly felt, to them, like any other year on the perpetual calendar. But 1951 was the last year of the old America—the pre-television America that was local and specific, the America in which a town's boundaries really were more or less binding.

Soon enough the country would be wired and linked, not only by television signals but by the interstate highway system. In 1951 the television explosion had not quite happened, radio still ruled; in 1951 the way you got from one town to another was on two-lane highways. The downtown movie houses were still crowded every night of the week, the evening papers still hit the front stoops just before dinner, and a hometown felt like both a home and a town, constant and fixed. Within five years everything would change—within five years antennas would jut from every roof, government engineers would be out with surveying equipment plotting freeways that would connect every town.

Within five years 1951 would seem as distant as 1917. And we would never know.

You think *you* feel old? Consider this:

Your parents have a 50-year-old child.

Think how that makes *them* feel.

The reason there has been such a groaning grinding of gears during the transition from our parents' generation of presidents to our generation of presidents has little to do with standard politics. It's much more elemental.

Think back to the first time your father handed you the

keys to his car. Such a simple, seemingly casual gesture, yet one fraught with deeply hidden emotions on both sides. Is he really ready to hand them over? Are you really ready to take them? Neither of you truly knows.

Now it's not the car. It's the White House.

("He would keep his eyes on the speedometer," David Eisenhower said. "He didn't know if I had proper road judgment.")

From our parents' America to ours, we have seen the profound change from "to grandmother's house we go" to the advent of grandparents' rights groups: organizations founded with the goal of helping grandmothers and grandfathers be allowed to see the grandchildren who are being kept away from them by angry ex-daughters-in-law and ex-sons-in-law.

And those grandchildren, caught in the middle of this, will soon enough be parents themselves.

I have a friend who, when he is happy or when he has had some drinks with his dinner, chortles. That's the only word for it—he chortles, and it is the same chortle I used to hear from his father, who is now dead. When I tell him that the sound is the same, he denies it.

I have another friend who, out of nowhere, will often fall silent and stare off into the middle distance, as if some private thought has just occurred. I used to see his father, now dead, do the same thing. When I tell him about this, he says he does not remember his dad doing that.

I have another friend whose third wife reminds me almost exactly of his mother when we were teenagers. I have not said anything to him about this.

Perhaps this is how it is destined to happen. Perhaps we

have no say. Perhaps, at 50, we must become our parents whether we wish to or not.

I have a woman friend who says to me that the trucks on the highways—the high speeds at which they drive, the closeness with which they tailgate—are frightening to her. She says she never used to notice the trucks, they never used to scare her, but now they do.

I tell her that she sounds like what our mothers used to sound like, complaining about the trucks. She says she knows it. She says that is what bothers her.

I was supposed to go to my father's house. He is 81.

On the way over, I stopped at a grocery store and picked up some things I thought he might like. From the store's frozen confectioneries department I got him a couple of Drumsticks and a couple of ice cream sandwiches.

I did not buy them with any sense of irony. They are the same things he used to bring to me. I thought he might like them. He did.

When we were growing up, our parents—and, by extension, we—had three basic times and places where each day we received the news of the world:

Morning paper. Evening paper. Walter Cronkite (or Huntley-Brinkley).

The rest of the day, with the exception of a few minutes on the car radio, was news-free. Today the news comes at everyone from all directions, all the time. The phrase "24-hour news channel" applies not only to specific broadcast entities, but to that expansive and gridlocked all-media channel that is our way of living, plugged into our ears and eyes and brains, ceaselessly delivering nonstop news.

And we are beginning to sense that those twenty-three hours without news—the twenty-three hours of each day when we used to be blissfully oblivious to the world's pressing events—were important to us. Having those twenty-three newsless hours mattered. More and more, we seem to be feeling the effects of not having those twenty-three hours.

Your parents were drawn to Wolfie's as if the place were a giant magnet.

And it was a magnet, in a way—a magnet made up of pastrami, chopped liver, blueberry cheesecake, corned beef, coleslaw, potato salad, Swiss cheese, chocolate sodas . . .

Wolfie's happened to be located in Miami Beach, but even if your parents had never been in Florida, they flocked to all the many variations of Wolfie's in the towns where they did vacation. No one had yet figured out just how unhealthy all that Wolfie's-style food was for a person, so your parents could go there with an absence of remorse, and an abundance of fun. What they didn't know couldn't hurt them.

And even if it could—even if it did—were they so much worse off at 50 than you are at 50—you, a person who somberly knows you should avoid a place like Wolfie's as if it may blow up at any second?

If that's so, then why, having read those selections from the Wolfie's menu three paragraphs ago, do you want so badly to go there right this minute?

The generational difference:

When our parents noticed the print in advertisements and phone-book listings getting smaller, they knew it was time to go get their eyes checked.

When we notice the print getting smaller, we offendedly think, "Don't they know better than to make the type so tiny? How can they expect us to give them our business if we can't even read the listings?''

Our parents' world was in large measure a world of costumes.

The suit-and-tie, dresses-and-nylons America through which they walked had a different texture than the backwards-baseball-caps, baggy-jeans America we live in today. Obviously, beneath the surface of their more formal America, plenty of troubles were hidden. But might the formal costumes have helped just a little bit? Might the costumes, with their studied civility, have done their measure to keep the lid on, back in those days when men and women wore suits and dresses even to the ballpark?

Think of blue jeans, and the presidents of our lifetime. Truman in jeans? No. Eisenhower? No. Kennedy? Not that we ever saw. LBJ? Maybe, on the ranch, but the predominant memory is of baggy fishing-and-hunting pants. Nixon? Not a chance. Ford? Nope.

Carter? Yes—there it began. Reagan? Yes—even he, on his days off. Bush? Not really—a step back toward Nixon. Clinton? Yes, of course—even getting off Air Force One after certain trips. Does it matter? Probably no more than the suits and ties at the ballpark mattered. In setting a tone, establishing an atmosphere. Constructing the civilized veneer, so thin at times.

But even the costumes, when they change, remain costumes.

Our fathers may have had to model themselves after the Man in the Gray Flannel Suit. Conformity never disappears, though; it merely puts on a new uniform. The man or woman of 50 who today must decide just how casual to be on Casual Friday, just how far to dress down on Dress-Down

Day at the office—those decisions are no less vexing. Casual Friday may come cloaked in a smile, but beneath the golf shirts and Levi's are still the men—and women—whose nervous forebears at the office hid inside those suits of gray flannel.

The clothing worn by the customers at the baseball parks may, indeed, change; the ballparks themselves, and the men on the diamonds, may change. But there are moments when those kinds of changes seem very minor.

I gave my parents tickets to a spring-training baseball game. This was during the spring that Michael Jordan was trying out for the Chicago White Sox; the ballpark was sold out every day.

My parents happened to be vacationing in the area, so I gave them the tickets—box seats. I was covering the game from the press box, and I saw them arrive—early, as is their custom—and take their seats in the sun.

It was a broiling Florida afternoon. I watched them sitting there, and I found myself paying more attention to them than to the batting practice that was going on. Each had been through a spell of bad health, and I kept my eyes on them as if by doing so, I could make sure that the sun was not getting to be too much.

Just before the game began, some guys in their 20s, wearing tank tops and shorts, beer cups in their hands, took the seats in front of them. From the press box I could see that the guys were already on the way to being drunk; the game started and I saw them hollering animatedly and sloppily toward the players, and I tried to read my mother's expression, tried to see how my dad was reacting.

I knew this vigilance wasn't necessary. My parents can take care of themselves; this was hardly their first sporting event—they have been going to Ohio State football games every autumn since before I was born. And it's not like the young men in front of them were serial killers—they were just loud and boisterous ballpark drunks, like you see in every ballpark.

But I felt responsible. In the press box, I watched my mom and dad in the implacable sun, asked myself if I had really done them such a favor by giving them the tickets. Jordan came to bat and promptly struck out. Somehow I thought that was my fault, too. The guys in front of them ordered another round of beers, and the temperature in the ballpark rose, and I was the parent, sitting in the press box watching and wishing I could make this day a little different. Even though there was nothing so wrong with the day, I wished I could make it better.

Like the father who sits in a ballpark with his son, looking at the boy but also seeing himself as a boy, looking at his boy looking at the ball game and being both the father who is there today and the son who used to be there with his own father forty years before, being the father and the child all at once, and that fact being so much more important than the game out on the diamond . . .

Like that father—like all of those fathers, in every ballpark—I looked down from the press box, and in the sixth inning, when my parents left the park, I could at last relax and pay attention to the contest down below.

"Got him!" yells the child with excitement, talking to a screen.

At 50 you see the children sitting in front of the television screens by themselves, playing video games. They seem to be enjoying it.

The essential difference between those solitaire video games and the board games (Monopoly, Clue) that you as a child used to play with your brothers and sisters, mother

and father, is the same difference between the family dinners you used to have, and the families today eating their
dinners at different hours, spread all over the house. Everyone still gets fed (everyone still plays a game). Yet . . .

Whenever, at 50, you hear your inner voice encouraging
you—telling you that you should be angry because someone is not treating you with respect, or that you can do
better at your job, or that you shouldn't feel left out because you're better than the people who are ignoring
you . . .

Whenever you hear that voice, the voice you can't get rid
of, is it really your voice? It sounds like you—it sounds like
your voice—but, all this time later, you have a hunch that it
is the voice of your parents, urging you on.

For the first time in your life you have this thought:

Do your parents need money?

They have never said it. And you ask yourself: Would
they? If it were true? And how do you possibly raise the
subject?

You stop to think about whether there are still any bad
influences on you at 50.

That's what—and who—your parents always blamed all
your troubles on—bad influences. It was their way of telling
you (or maybe telling themselves) that you (and they) were
all right. If things were going wrong, it was because of the
bad influences.

If it ever was true, does the possibility even exist for it to
be true today? At your age, can anyone still influence you in
a bad way? Or have you been influenced all you can ever be
influenced, both good and bad?

Besides, some of the people they thought were the worst

influences ended up influencing you in some of the most wholesome ways.

Elvis, for instance, the one your parents always thought was the most terrible influence of all:

Could they have had any idea that it was Elvis, and Elvis alone, who is the reason you call every adult you meet "sir" or "ma'am"? Even adults who are younger than you? That Elvis—Elvis, of all people—turned out to be the person who influenced you into being so polite?

When every house had a sewing machine, you now believe, the national fabric itself seemed just a little bit stronger.

Would you, today, ever allow a milkman to do what your parents allowed the milkman to do every day?

To enter your house in pre-dawn darkness, while everyone in the family is asleep, and to go through the refrigerator replenishing the dairy goods? Give him the key to the house, knowing that he would come and go by the time the sun was up? And not think for a second that such an arrangement was unusual?

Because it wasn't.

Among the many reasons that the drive-in movies of your parents' generation—so plentiful and so popular—are now an endangered species is this:

The thought of parking with strangers in a dark, remote field on the outskirts of town seems, at best, ill-advised. To feel truly sanguine about such a place, you'd need the National Guard patrolling the pebble-paved aisles.

Who knows who those other people are, out there in the dark?

(Maybe your milkman.)

· · ·

There are certain things from your parents' world, though, that no one misses. Not even for a second.

Take clotheslines.

There is probably not an American alive who feels even a single pang of regret over the disappearance of clotheslines and clothespins. For starters, it didn't work that well—automatic dryers do the job quicker and better. And as far as privacy goes, and lack of it, right down to bras and underpants: Where do you think they got the phrase "airing your dirty laundry"?

Find someone who says they're nostalgic for clotheslines and you've found someone with too much time on their hands.

"You're keeping Kodak in business," says the woman, 55, to her daughter, 30, who is taking snapshot after snapshot of her babies.

There's a novel in that joking sentence—a novel of family history, and saved memories, and who's the boss and how people talk to each other and love each other. "You're keeping Kodak in business," said as a chiding joke, as she watches her daughter snap the shutter again and preserve these moments forever.

When you think about your parents' mortality, the thing that strikes you as being most important—the thing that is basic, at the top of the list of what counts in your life—is this:

After they are gone, who is going to be angry at you when you've done something wrong, and who is going to be proud of you when you've done something right? There are other people who will fill those roles, and whose anger or whose pride will matter to you. But who will make you feel quite the same way as when the reactions—bad or good— are coming from them?

No one. And you know it.

8

The Ladder with No Top Rung

When a person gets his or her first full-time job right out of school, the idea of a career really does seem like a ladder— like a ladder stretching so high and so far you couldn't even begin to see the top as you put your foot on that first rung.

At 50, you see it somewhat differently. You've been on that ladder for a long time now, and your view of it has little in common with the view you had on that first day of work.

When a boss puts up a memo on the bulletin board these days, congratulating the staff for a great job on a recent big project, you now realize that it has almost nothing to do with those of you who are on that staff.

When you were 22, you would see a note like that and fight the temptation to take it off the board, photocopy it, and send it to your parents to show them how well you were doing. You had been a part of a project that had been carried out in spectacular fashion. Look—the big boss was saying so, right in this official staff memo.

Today you understand: The boss is only congratulating himself. At his level, that's what he's in the position to do: declare victory via staff memo. By writing and posting the memo, he is announcing that all of his decisions (including the decision to hire all of you) were smart decisions. There are few people in the company with the power to judge him, so he judges himself—and reaches a verdict that he is a very fine executive, indeed.

He can prove it—look, it's right there on the board.

When I was a beginning newspaper reporter, I was assigned to do a story on Jack E. Leonard, the famous comedian known for his rapid-fire insults of the audience.

He was a regular guest on *The Tonight Show,* and there probably wasn't a person in the country who didn't know who he was. A bald, rotund, barking-voiced presence on-stage, he was the picture of self-confidence and swagger. He was in town for a nightclub appearance, and I was sent down to talk to him.

When I got to the nightclub, an hour or so before show-time, I was surprised to find him not in his dressing room, but sitting in the very back row of tables, in shadows. I joined him to find a quite morose fellow. He was worried that no one—or at least very few people—would show up.

So as we sat there together and the customers trickled in, Jack E. Leonard counted the house. Literally—he was keeping track of the actual number of people at the tables. On nights when he was on *The Tonight Show* with Johnny Carson, he was seen by millions upon millions of people, but this was different; at this nightclub he was able to quantify the number of people who felt he was worth spending their money on, and the thought seemed to worry him.

Maybe it never really goes away, whether your business is comedy or manufacturing auto parts. You count the house every day of your business life—whether you can see the customers, like Jack E. Leonard could in his line of work, or you are made aware of the customers strictly by sales figures. But you are always counting the house, and however many miles of success you may have had yesterday does not guarantee an inch of success today.

Or so it seems. That night with Jack E. Leonard, his mood grew brighter as the house did, in fact, begin to fill as showtime grew closer. Later a man who knew him told me that Leonard always did this—every night he would sit there thinking that the customers wouldn't come, and only when he could see for himself that they were there would he go back to his dressing room and prepare for his entrance.

All of which, the next night, would mean nothing. He'd be out there early again, worrying and counting. Apparently it's a feeling that many men and women, at 50, still not certain the customers are always going to be out there, can identify with. Makes you think about what it will feel like on the day you finally decide you don't have to do this—when you're sure enough of your business that you don't need to count the house. If such a day, in fact, ever comes, to anyone.

And if that day of complete and total business self-confidence never does quite arrive, it's probably because your view at 50 of the world of business has just about nothing in common with the view you had when you were a kid.

Back then, the idea of business was represented by the drugstore over on Main Street, clean and well stocked and smelling vaguely of sweet disinfectant, open every day, the place where your parents got their prescriptions filled and you checked out the new supply of bubble gum cards and magazines and school notebooks. You knew the man who owned the place, and the guy behind the pharmacy window, and JoAnn, the woman at the cash register. It was just *there*—that was the function of businesses, to be there for you and for the town. It didn't really occur to you, when you were a kid, that the people who ran the place had to stay in business, and that there were all kinds of uncertainties involved in that. Even on days when you and your sister were the only people wandering around the drugstore, looking at stuff, it didn't strike you that if you were the only people in there (and you weren't going to spend any money), then maybe the owner had the right to be a little worried.

Now, you think that kind of thought all the time—not only about your own business, but about every business you deal with. Now, if you could transport yourself back in time to that drugstore on Main Street, you would undoubtedly do the calculations in your head: If they're bringing so little money in, then how much longer can the owner pay the pharmacist? How's he going to keep paying JoAnn? The part of business that was invisible to you when you were young—the business part of business—is all you can see now. The shelves with the boxes of No. 2 pencils and pink erasers are full, yes, but if no one's buying them in this store, how are the suppliers getting paid?

When you and your sister would walk out of the store, sometimes there would be no one left inside. No one but the owner, the pharmacist, and JoAnn. That felt fine to you, when you were a kid—sort of private and fun. But when you were a kid you never looked back through the store's glass door after you were gone, to see them standing there.

• • •

That person? The one you resent because he has gone further than you, is bigger in your business than you are, has
more money than you do—based on what you consider to
be much less talent and intelligence than you have?

There's someone who feels exactly the same way about
you.

It's something to keep in mind while on mid-ladder: that
as unfair as you believe someone else's success to be, some
other person probably believes that your success and position are just as undeserved. And as sure as you are about
the failings of the person above you on the ladder, the
person beneath you is just as sure about your failings.

If someone could harness all the energy expended by
people on the ladder being angry and bitter about the ones
on the rungs just above—energy those people expend while
at the same time ignoring the good luck that has placed
them on the rung above those just below . . .

But then, that's the energy that keeps you going. Until
you begin to figure out, at 50, the absurdity of it all.

You tend to get so caught up in your business that if someone were to ask you to answer very quickly, without pausing
to think, what month it is, you might not be able to do it.

You've been going over the figures for last quarter's sales
results; you've been attending meetings making plans for
the fall presentations. Those months both past and future
you have been quite involved in. But this month—right
now, today—is something that doesn't feel as present-tense
as it should.

The months are interchangeable, and the month you are
living in today doesn't have much meaning. Which may be
all right for your business, but it can't be much good for
your life.

•   •   •

"What's he going to do? Do you know? He always thought he was going to take over."

I heard two men talking, and one of them said that to the other. It was one of those passages that didn't need an antecedent—everything you needed to know about the person they were discussing was contained in those seventeen words. At 50, you hear those words and you are immersed in certain truths about the man who is the subject of their conversation, and about them, and about every person who ever started up the ladder all those many years ago. About you . . .

The counting-the-house phenomenon apparently never ends. Ever.

I have seen it at funerals. Really. People counting the house—adding up the number of mourners, as if that offers some objective answer to the success of the deceased's life. As if it's still, when the person is dead, some kind of competition.

"Come on," you think, watching the survivors counting the number of people in the pews. "Stop that." But there's no stopping it. Life ends, and the scoreboard stays lit.

The truth that, at 50, you become finally aware of is that there is no top rung to that ladder you've been on. If you're waiting to reach the top rung, you can forget it, because it doesn't exist.

When, many years after that evening with Jack E. Leonard, I made it to *The Tonight Show* myself, I got to the NBC studios in Burbank earlier than I had been told to arrive. I guess that, without knowing it, to me *The Tonight Show* had always represented the top rung. If you ever got there, then there would be no need for any more striving. That's what had puzzled me, at 22, about Jack E. Leonard counting the house. Why should he need to count the house? He's already won the game—he's a guy from *The Tonight Show*. No counting necessary.

I arrived at the NBC studios and I put my stuff in the dressing room they'd given me, and I walked around and asked directions until I was backstage on the big set, behind the curtain. The audience had not been allowed in yet, and would not be for another hour or so. I asked a stagehand if I could walk out and sit in the seat where I'd be sitting later.

He gave me a quizzical look; being here was his daily job, routine to him, and I was treating the whole thing like it was a transatlantic crossing. Which, in a way, it was. He said sure; he said go ahead out there. I walked across that little path from the curtains to the desk and the chairs, thinking the whole way that the floor was slick beneath my feet and that I might slip and fall when the time came to do it for real, and what would that be like—falling on the *Tonight Show* floor in front of the whole country. I got to the seat— the John Wayne seat, I couldn't stop asking myself what I was doing in that seat next to the desk, this was where John Wayne used to sit, it was where John Wayne belonged, not me—and I looked out at the empty seats, at the technicians getting the cameras and lights ready for the evening's show (one more evening at work for all of them).

Doc Severinsen had arrived, and was over in the band area, doing something, and he waved hello. I tried to take it all in. This was the top rung, right now. This was not last quarter's sales figures, this was not next winter's projected plans—this was happening now. Try to live inside it, right now, I told myself.

Yet later that evening, when the show was over—when my time in the John Wayne chair was done and the music played and the credits rolled—there was this feeling of emptiness. Immediately—the emptiness started while I was still sitting there. There is no top rung that makes you feel that the climb is finished. Wherever you think the finish line may be, you will be wrong. If the top rung really did feel like the top rung, it would be good and it would be bad. Good because it would finally settle you, let you exhale. Bad because it would do away with ambition. If what you thought was the finish line really was, then what would you do after that?

Walking out to the John Wayne chair before the audience was there had felt more thrilling than the show itself, because when I was out there alone, it hadn't happened yet. The anticipation was still intoxicating. It's like the Christmas feeling: It is the strongest on the days before Christmas, when you're still waiting for the big day. On Christmas morning itself, when all the packages have been opened, there's that letdown. Until you tell yourself that in another year, it will be Christmas Eve again. Then you can work yourself back to excitement and hope.

At least you could as a kid. At 50 you keep the lesson in mind. And, even knowing the top rung is illusory, you keep pulling yourself toward it. Because there is no alternative to that pursuit, or at least none you are aware of, so you continue on your climb, not knowing what lies ahead. Maybe John Wayne did. But maybe not.

Your whole business life you have tried to be a good employee—to do a job that will please the people for whom you work.

And then, sometime around 50, a different question occurs to you: Am I a good boss? Do the people beneath me in the company's structure think of me that way?

It was always the other way around—you always thought about whether you were good enough to satisfy the people you worked for. And one day, without you noticing, you crossed the invisible line, and became the person others hoped was evaluating them with approval. It's an odd thing to ponder, and there's no one you can talk to about it. Because you're the boss.

One of the absolute truths about being 50 at work is that never again can you be thought of as an up-and-comer.

Not in any way. Not in any profession or field of endeavor. Not by any manner of defining such things. Even if, inside yourself, you are full of the same drive and energy that fueled you at 23, you are no longer eligible. You can be good at what you do; you can be successful. But a door has closed.

You can't be a hotshot.

We seldom stop to think about how dependent we are on the "of the" crutch.

We have used it every day of our working lives, on almost every business call we make: "Hello, I'm Joe Smith of the . . ." And we insert the name of our company.

Without the "of the," we are as naked and alone as if we were without our clothes. The traumatic part of changing jobs—or of being fired—is based in large part on the absence of the "of the," and how much all of us count on it without realizing it.

Even when executives rise high enough that the "of the" is left unsaid—when the network of a person's business contacts is so well established that the person's name alone gets him through to whomever he wants to speak to—the "of the" is implied and real. Which is why, when the CEO of General Mills or IBM retires, he may get a multimillion-dollar bonus package and stocks that will provide for him until his dying day, but there is still a void, and it's the void brought on by the loss of the "of the." People discover that they need the "of the" in their lives just as much as they need the salary and the benefits.

Without the "of the," you're just you again.

Speaking of businesspeople feeling naked and without their clothes:

It's not a bad technique to use when you have to go into a pressure-filled meeting with a high-powered, no-nonsense, intimidating group of people.

During the meeting, look at them and think of them naked. Beneath those suits, below those grim faces, they're just a bunch of naked people. When things get heated and tense, and they're making an agitated point to you, picture them without their clothes on. It will relax you and make the whole business exercise seem a little more pleasingly funny. Won't change the outcome of the meeting, of course—but it will lighten your mood.

On the other hand, some of these intimidating bosses actually *do* like to be naked with their subordinates. These are the people who go to health clubs, saunas, steam rooms, and the like with the people who work for them. The kind of self-confidence that allows a boss to do this—to sit around naked with the people who work for him—is frightening. You should go to any means to avoid this. An unbreakable rule, especially at 50, is: Don't be naked with your boss.

In your 20s and 30s and 40s, you used to hear about contemporaries—people you knew, people your own age—making it big: getting great jobs, becoming millionaires, being named presidents of their companies. There was always an almost palpable jolt when you heard those things.

At 50, you are beginning to feel the same jolt when you hear about people—people you know, people your own

age—losing it. Losing their jobs, having their money wiped
out, tumbling back to the bottom. People who used to be in
power, now looking for any job they can find, sometimes
having to settle for something menial.

The jolt you feel, now as then, is a manifestation of what
you are thinking: "*That?* Happened to *him?*" You felt oddly
shaken by someone else's good news before; you feel oddly
shaken by someone else's bad news now. What the two have
in common is this:

It didn't happen to you.

But it could.

Traversing the long span of a career, it is advisable to keep
the Ron Allen Factor in mind.

Ron Allen, for many years, was the name used by local
disc jockeys and radio newscasters in cities and towns
throughout America. The name served two purposes. It was
flat and non-ethnic, so listeners in any town could tune to
Ron Allen—whoever he happened to be—on their radio
dials, and accept him as a bland, white-bread part of their
lives. The other purpose, though, was just as significant:

Local radio station executives, as often as not, were the
ones who named their on-air performers Ron Allen. The
broadcaster didn't come to town with the idea of being Ron
Allen—he was persuaded to be Ron Allen by his new boss.
The boss knew that if this particular Ron Allen didn't work
out, he could always try another Ron Allen later.

The Ron Allen Factor is a good thing to be aware of even
when you're 50 years old, the chief officer of your company,
and have never been in a radio studio in your life. Because
it is a prime example of how we're all interchangeable, no
matter how irreplaceable to our companies we fool ourselves into thinking we are. It all cycles around; we're all, in
one way or another, filling slots. There was someone in the

slot before we got here; there will be someone in the slot after we're gone.

We're all Ron Allen. Signing on, signing off.

Or we're Fred Whiting.

Fred Whiting was a wonderful journalism professor I had in college. He told me a story when I was 19—a story the power of which at the time I suppose I didn't fully comprehend.

He said that after he had been teaching college journalism students for years, he got a call from one of the big Chicago television stations. They had an opening for a TV sportscaster; they had heard that Fred had a good voice and a strong verbal delivery, and they wanted to know if he'd be interested in coming downtown to apply for the job.

He was interested, all right. He'd been a professor for a long time. The idea of doing something new—something like this—appealed to him.

So he went downtown to the television station, and he walked in. And he found out that he would be auditioning directly against some men who were his former students. Some of them, in fact, had very recently been his students.

He looked around at the other men in the room—men he had taught the business—and he was mortified. Mortified and hurt. No one had told him this. No one had told him that he was going to be judged against younger men who would not be in this room were it not for the classes they had taken from him. And that the chances were very good that, because of the cosmetic requirements of television, he would lose.

He left. He didn't try out. He walked out and went back to the campus. His anger and his embarrassment stayed with him, though. They could have told him. That was the thing, he said: They could have told him.

At 19, I thought I could grasp the meaning of his story.
Today, I know I can.

Somewhere in your house, you probably have your old class
pictures—your kindergarten class picture, your third-grade
class picture, all of you in the class standing in rows, smiling
toward the camera, your teacher to the side.

Those class pictures are a part of American life. But no
one ever arranges to take class pictures at work. The people
with whom you work every day are actors and bit players in
some of the most vivid scenes of your adult years, yet it
never gets captured on film. Would you not be interested in
having an office picture from your class of '71, your class of
'73, your class of '76? Just a group shot, to remind you of
who you were—and the people who were a part of that?

It's a picture that never gets taken. We're supposed to be
too sophisticated to want such things, once we leave school
and go to work.

One of the things to watch out for at the office—although it
eventually becomes all but unavoidable—is that, at 50, you
tend to lean on your veteran status.

Meaning that you begin to take things as your due—that
you believe you have a right to certain perquisites, certain
assignments, a certain deference, because you have been a
part of the company for so long. On paper, maybe that is
accurate—you may even have it written down in a contract.
But falling back on your pecking rights as a company veteran is completely different from showing the enthusiasm
and energy you did when you were new there, a person with
no inherent pecking rights at all, trying to prove yourself.

Now you feel that you have those certain things coming
to you. Like interest that you've earned in a savings account.

But inside, you know that there is no such thing as an interest-bearing account in the office atmosphere of today. If such accounts ever existed, they have long ago been closed. Insufficient funds.

At some point on the way to 50, some people veer off in one direction while others wouldn't even think of it.

I was staying at a hotel where a guest complained that his wife was coughing all the time because of construction going on on the property. He said he was sure it was because of a reaction she was having to the fuel oil used in the construction machinery.

He told the manager of the hotel that he and his wife had planned this trip for months, and that he would take the hotel to court because the construction was ruining the vacation. The manager didn't buy this—no one else at the hotel was saying they were getting sick because of the machinery—but, to head off legal difficulties, the manager made arrangements with another hotel for the man and his wife to move and get five free days and nights. It just seemed like less trouble.

And perhaps it was. But at what point does a person like that guest stop being the kid he was, a kid to whom such a thought would never occur—threatening legal action over machine oil at a hotel—and become a tough enough businessman to turn it into a free vacation? Quite apart from who was right and who was wrong in this specific instance, what happens to turn a person into that?

It doesn't happen to everyone—if it did, all the rest of us would be complaining and getting free vacations all the time. The scary thing is that whatever it was that made it happen to this man, it probably turned him into a big success at whatever it is he does.

•   •   •

Every guy who has a line of dialogue in a TV commercial
wanted at one point in his life to be Tom Cruise or Jack
Nicholson. Every woman who has a walk-on wanted to be
Meryl Streep. Every person who plays the piano at a wedding reception wanted to be John Lennon. Each of them
studied hard and worked and worked.

This is not something you necessarily want to spend too
much time thinking about at 50. The day will probably
come for all of us when we learn that we're not going to get
the top job. It's no longer a case of ambition or persever-
ance, of talent or of sticking with your plan. There comes a
day when we learn that it's not going to happen—whatever
the "it" is leaves the picture.

And that day can, oddly enough, be a rather good day.
Because on that day you reach a new level in your life. What
you have ended up having in your career is not exactly what
you had in mind when you started out. That can be a free-
ing revelation—and how you deal with it from that point
on, how happy you make yourself in light of this new knowledge, may turn out to be the most significant definer of
yourself you have ever had to create. Use it well.

Yet success is not always easily defined. I once met Tram-
mell Crow, the largest landlord in America. Crow's personal
wealth, at the time, was estimated to be in excess of $500
million.

I found him sitting at a desk out in a bullpen area of his
corporate headquarters, surrounded by other employees.
He might have been a long-tenured bookkeeper, plugging
away in the midst of younger workers. I asked him where his
own office was. He said he didn't have one. I asked him
why.

"I don't know," he said. "I've never had a private office
in my life. I like it this way."

"But what if you want privacy?" I said.

"I don't want privacy," he said. "Look, I don't even have a locked desk. There's no lock on it. If people want to know what's in my desk, they're welcome to look. The way I figure it, the more they know, the better.

"I tell my assistants that if a letter to me is marked 'Personal,' open that letter first. I have no such thing as private mail. And as far as a private office goes, I'm certainly not going to start now."

So maybe, at 50, that's the business goal to reach for—no office, no privacy, no locks on your desk. Or at least the psychological equivalent of that. The status that comes with the freedom to reject status.

No need to hurry with any of this, though. No reason to think you're falling behind. Just because Jonas Salk was 38 when he developed the polio vaccine, there's no need for the rest of us to fret about whether we've been spending our time wisely.

Think of it this way: Abraham Lincoln was 52 when he became president, so we've got plenty of time to catch up, right? Franklin Roosevelt was 51 when he entered the White House and began to lead the nation out of the Great Depression—no reason for us to feel any undue pressure. George Washington? He was 57 when he became president. The Father of His Country, at 57 . . .

Hey, we'll get right on it. As soon as we get around to cleaning out the garage.

9

Uncle Phil in Your Bedroom Mirror

One of the most intriguing parts of being 50 is how much of the time you still feel like a kid. That's not a kid looking back at you from the mirror in the morning; that's certainly not a kid who feels the creakiness and strains in your muscles and bones. Yet whoever the person who lives inside your 50-year-old body is, that person is pretty young.

And, you must admit, not always that overwhelmingly mature, either. Anytime you are served mashed potatoes, for example—anytime, at a restaurant, a waiter tells you that one of the dishes you may choose with your dinner is mashed potatoes—you hear, in your head, the opening few seconds of that old Dartells song from 1963:

"Mashed potatoes, yeah . . ."

As clear as if some band was playing it in the room where you're eating dinner: You hear the organ wailing, and the singer's high-pitched voice:

"Mashed potatoes, yeah . . ."

You silently ask yourself whether other people all around the world have this thought whenever mashed potatoes are offered. Whether the men in their business suits, the women in their conservative dresses, sit there looking at the menu, while in their heads . . .

"Mashed potatoes, yeah . . ."

You look up toward the waiter and say, in a dignified voice:

"I believe I'll have the mashed potatoes."

And it's not just a question of potatoes that are mashed, or of that particular song in your head. Whatever you look like on the outside, that person inside is still moving around to the sounds of the first songs you loved. The other day I heard the Supremes' 1964 hit "Where Did Our Love Go" on an oldies station, and immediately and involuntarily I reached my right arm toward the ceiling and started making banging motions in a downward direction. I did it without knowing why I was doing it.

It took me a second to figure out the reason. That summer when "Where Did Our Love Go" first came out, my friends and I cruised around the streets of our hometown in a blue Ford that was owned by one of us—a guy whose first name was Allen. Every time that song would come on the radio, with its insistent first words—"Baby, baby . . ."—we would reach out the window and bang on the top of the car roof. Right in time with those two words—"Baby, baby . . ."

Here I was, more than thirty years later, banging on an invisible roof as I heard the words. Just as an experiment, I called another of my old friends—a guy who had been in that car all that summer—and asked him the question. I said: "What do the first words of 'Where Did Our Love Go' make you feel like doing?"

He paused for a moment, making himself recall the song, as if his mind was a jukebox (which, of course, all of our minds are). I heard him say the two words, flatly, without inflection: "Baby, baby . . ."

Then he answered my question:

"Bang on the roof of Allen's car."

Right. At 50.

We'd better get used to the fact that this is it—that our Cole Porters and George Gershwins are the people who wrote and sang "Harry the Hairy Ape" and "Big Girls Don't Cry" and "My Boyfriend's Back" and "Leader of the Pack." No offense to the memories (not to mention the talents) of Mr. Porter and Mr. Gershwin, but a person's old standards are the songs that came out of the radio when he or she was young—they don't feel like standards at the time, they become standards by default, by virtue of simply having been there.

And for us, it wasn't "Night and Day" or "You're the Top" or "Rhapsody in Blue." For us—for better or for worse—those standards-in-waiting happened to be "Wipe Out" and "Duke of Earl" and "Walk Like a Man" and "Hello Mudduh, Hello Fadduh." Those are the spurs to unleashing the floodgates of our memories.

Those television commercials trying to get us to order CD collections of old hits—the CDs that are packaged by Time-Life (a weird-enough concept—*Time* magazine was the dominant tut-tutting national voice dismissing rock and roll music when we were young, and now its parent company is endeavoring to re-sell the songs to us) . . .

Those television commercials show people talking fondly about the music, and how much it meant to them, as the

800 number flashes on the screen. And the people who are reminiscing—the actors hired by Time-Life to lure us to buy the CDs—are like Grandpa and Grandma. You stop for a second and ask yourself why these particular actors are the ones they hired—old people like that.

And then, of course, you realize that the grandfathers and grandmothers in the commercials (young grandfathers and grandmothers, to be sure, but Gramps and Granny nevertheless) are your contemporaries. That's why they're on the screen—they are warm, weathered, settled in, they are the people who first heard those songs in 1958 and 1962 and 1964. They, and you.

The voices of the unseen singers of the songs as the titles roll by in the commercials are young voices—their voices were frozen in time the day their records were released. And as the grandparently actors and actresses reminisce about the music ("Sweet Little Sheila," "Breaking Up Is Hard to Do," "Sugar Shack"), they might as well be talking about the songs of Glenn Miller or the Dorsey Brothers. Which, in a sense, they are.

All of which is a part of the funny emotional bizarreness of 50. The first time anyone brought it up directly to me—the fact that 50 was on its way—was when an old friend (the same one who got the right answer about banging his hand on the car roof) called me and said, "Do you know what's going to happen?"

He said it with a smile in his voice, like he was about to tell me some warped new joke he'd just heard. "Do you know what's going to happen?"—in the kind of wry tone that's setting you up for a punch line.

But what he said was, "We're going to be 50." Like indeed it was a joke—the unspoken part was, "What a stupid, crazy joke, and there's nothing we can do about it, is there?'' Not a thing serious or sober about the way he said it—this was not his father's voice, speaking in deep inflections about reaching a landmark in the journey through life. This was the voice of a person who has just spoken to the kid who's renting the apartment inside of him, and has gotten the news that the kid is about to celebrate having been around for half a century.

And what would you like with that birthday cake, sir?

"Mashed potatoes, yeah . . .''

The dichotomies inherent in all this present themselves to you at unexpected moments.

Your 5-year-old niece is visiting, and she's showing you her doll catalog. She turns the pages of the catalog for you, pointing out the different dolls and telling you their names, and you intentionally mispronounce the names and get them wrong, which makes her laugh and correct you, then laugh harder and correct you again when you keep it up.

You're both laughing, having fun, and when she has to leave, she doesn't want to stop—the two of you are still making jokes about the names of the dolls.

And after she's gone you think:

The good part was all the laughter. All that joy.

The bad part is that you really don't want to be Uncle Phil, the odd and eccentric uncle who used to come to your house when you were a kid—Uncle Phil, the goofball who hid the nickels behind his ears and produced them as presents for you.

Doesn't matter what you want. In the car on her way home, you know she's laughing and talking about how that silly guy couldn't even get the names of the dolls right.

This is depressing. You *are* Uncle Phil.

•   •   •

You hear business executives talking about "key man insurance"—policies taken out by the corporations they work for, to provide coverage should something happen to the CEO.

The men who are talking about this are doing so in businesslike voices, but it's clear, beneath the words, that there is a certain pride involved. To be the key man—to be officially recognized as such, named in the insurance policy—is like wearing the captain's star on a high school letter sweater. There were lots of other players on the high school football team—but only one got to pin that gold star on his sweater.

You'd think, fifty years on, there would be a big difference between the two things. But there's not. The CEO can't wear a letter sweater to board-of-directors meetings. Being listed as the "key man" in the firm's insurance coverage will have to do. If only he could pin the policy to his suit lapel, so everyone could see it.

You're stopped at a traffic light and a car pulls up next to you and, just for a second, you have the urge to drag-race with the other driver as soon as the light turns green.

You have no idea where this notion came from. You look over at him, thinking about whether he's thinking it, too.

Probably not. The light turns, and you creep carefully along, merging with traffic on your way home.

Even at 50, your first boss is always, in your head, still your boss.

You've worked for several companies since you worked for that boss; in fact by now that boss may be dead. But the first person you worked for is still, in many ways, the one you are trying to please. No matter what has happened

since then to you, or to that first boss, that boss still holds a
certain authority over you.

It's a permutation of the same way your high school principal—someone who has absolutely nothing to say about
how you live your life now—continues to represent control
and power. In the years since you walked the hallways of
that principal's school, or were welcomed to the company
by that first boss, you have met any number of people who
are far more powerful than they. But it will never feel quite
the same as when you have never had a boss before—and
when you believe that boss's evaluation of you is the one
and only defining word about whether what you do has any
worth.

Someone sent me a copy of one of the old Dick and Jane
books.

Far more than any sense of cuteness or nostalgia, the
book conveyed a feeling of something deeply humbling.
This was the first Dick and Jane preprimer (*We Look and
See*); from the first word on the first page—"Look"—the
book represented the answer to one of life's mysteries. A
child is born, knowing nothing, unformed; when the child
is 6 years old, he or she somehow learns this miraculous
thing. The child learns to read. And the world opens up.

The Dick and Jane books, which were used to teach
young Americans to read in the 1930s, 1940s, 1950s, and
part of the 1960s, have gone out of print. They are no
longer found in American schools. To those of us who can
still remember our first teacher showing us that first word
on Page One of *We Look and See*—the excitement we felt,
knowing that word, suddenly knowing the shape of the
word, what it meant . . .

Well, miracle is not too strong a description. There were
only seventeen words in *We Look and See*—"look," "oh,"

"Jane," "see," "Dick," "funny," "Sally," "Puff," "jump,"
"run," "Spot," "come," "Tim," "up," "and," "go,"
"down"—and they were the key to everything. From the
day we first opened *We Look and See,* every time we learned a
new word, every time we could read a new story by ourselves, it would feel like a minor electrical charge. Every
day, for all the years in those early years of learning . . .
we would begin the day not knowing what certain words
looked like, and by the time school was out for the afternoon, we knew. Those words were ours, forever.

Everything that has come since, everything we have been
able to learn and achieve, started right there. At 50 there
are a lot of things to grin at and take lightly. Then you open
up an old schoolbook. And life, with all its possibilities,
becomes something quietly majestic.

On one of those Sunday morning television news shows, the
anchor is interviewing a newsmaker, and begins his question to the man by saying: "Mr. Ambassador . . ."

And as you're watching, you look at Mr. Ambassador and
see that he is younger than you are. This is becoming increasingly common—the Mr. Ambassadors of the world being your junior—and you ask yourself whether they are the
way they are, while you are the way you are, because they
really do have more gravity and weight, or whether they're
in on the joke, too? Whether when they get home from
being Mr. Ambassador they walk around in their underwear
and make wisecracks at the TV set and throw their empty
cans of pop at the wastebasket as if they're trying to hit an
NBA three-pointer—or instead sit around, their vested suits
still on, silently reading State Department cables beneath a
desk lamp.

It would be more disturbing to you if that's what they
did—if they stayed Mr. Ambassador even when the door was

locked to the outside world. I was in Washington on business, staying at the Ritz-Carlton, and I didn't feel like room
service, so I went downstairs to the Jockey Club and sat at a
table for one for dinner. At the table next to me were four
people who looked as if they had just come from Embassy
Row. A man at their table—younger than I—said to the
other three, "Well, I was telling His Highness last
week . . ."

Oh. So that's it. "I was telling His Highness . . ." It
made me think not only about the fellow who was saying it,
but about His Highness himself. When the door was locked
at the palace—whichever palace he happened to live in—
did His Highness, in a T-shirt and boxer shorts, play fetch
with the cat, using a pair of rolled-up socks? And if not, why
not?

Bob Halderman and John Ehrlichman? The tough guys of
the Nixon White House? The men who ran everything with
cold eyes and iron fists?

At 50, you are older than they were in that White House.
Just another little thing for you to think about on those days
when you can't figure out why the 50-year-old on the outside of you is in such conflict with the kid residing inside.
Haldeman and Ehrlichman, with their icy assurance and
absolute power—they were younger then than you are now.
Yikes.

You remember your first girlfriend's phone number, from
thirty-five years ago.

You remember your best friend's phone number, from
thirty-five years ago.

Some of the business phone numbers you call all the
time now, you can't remember without looking in the file.
You have to look them up every time.

While this may seem strange at first, it really isn't. It makes perfect sense. The reason you can't remember the business numbers now and you can still remember those numbers from long ago is that, at 50, the telephone numbers you call today are nowhere near as important to you as those other numbers were then.

And if you think those old-girlfriend phone numbers still resonate in your memory, ask yourself how Peggy Sue and Donna the Prima Donna and Runaround Sue feel.

They're out there, many of them—the girls whom the songs that filled our heads were written about. Some of them had the real names in the songs, some were merely inspirations, and as the years go by try to imagine what goes through them every time the radio plays those songs.

Sherry baby, and Sally who went 'round the roses, and Rhonda (whose help was needed), and Mrs. Brown's lovely daughter . . . they know who they are. If, at 50, when those songs come out of the radio, those now-grown-up girls don't tell the other people who happen to be in the room that the songs were written about them . . .

Well, can you blame them? Who would ever believe them?

At 50, when you run into old friends from when you were young, one of two things will happen.

With some of them, you will start to talk, and this wonderful thing will take place: You will find that it's as if you are continuing some conversation that was somehow interrupted thirty or forty years before, and now both of you are enthusiastically picking up on it, right where you left off. You'll finish each other's sentences, jump in with references to people and places, laugh at jokes only the two of you understand—you'll be much older than when the conversation started, so long ago, but that will hardly matter. If someone were to walk up to the two of you, that person would have no idea it had been so many years since you last spoke.

With other old acquaintances, though, you'll meet again, and the conversation will sound like an awkward business discussion. There will be long silences, and wordless second-guessing after every sentence—this person you once knew so well will be a stranger. It will be as if the passing years have acted as an eraser, getting rid of anything and everything you once had in common.

And the question is, what happened to make the people in that second group that way? It's too easy to say that they have matured and moved on. A lot of the people in the first group—the people with whom you seamlessly resume conversations from half a lifetime ago—are as mature and as steady as a person can get. So the question is, what happens to the other people, the ones who develop this sense of distance? Do they not remember the same things that you do—did something happen in their lives to do away with those things, replace them? If so, what was it that happened to them—and how can you avoid it?

Whatever it was that made some of these old friends so businesslike and arctic—how can you make sure that it never happens to you?

On this subject, one thing you should keep in mind is that the people who were jerks when you were younger can pretty much be counted on to remain jerks.

Example: I had done something to my back, knocking a disk out of place, and was wearing a neck brace. It hurt pretty much all the time; I was on a trip, and in an airport I unexpectedly ran into a man I had known many years before.

He asked me what had happened; I told him. I asked him if he ever had trouble with his back.

"No," he said. "I work out all the time. I keep myself in much too good a shape for something like that to happen."

And he was off. For a moment, I thought: Why did he say that? Of all the things he could have said, why did he say something as jerky as that?

And I knew the answer: because that's how he's always been. It's not that he's changed; it's just that his self-centeredness and lack of interest for other people's troubles have shifted to new areas of the human experience. At 12 he might have cut in line at the water fountain even though everyone else had been waiting. Approaching 50 he was saying that what someone else's pain meant to him was that he was smart enough to be above such things.

The most frustrating part is, he got the water exactly when he wanted it when he was 12—and his back probably never does hurt. Probably never will.

If sometimes, at 50, all of us seem somewhat emotionally limited, it may be because our generation of men was presented with certain archetypes when we were boys, and those archetypes were Roy Rogers, Bill Boyd and Gene Autry—the laconically omnipotent television cowboys we thought we were supposed to turn into. And our generation of women was presented with its own girlhood trio of archetypes: Barbara Billingsley, Jane Wyatt and Donna Reed—the sunny and uncomplaining television housewives American girls thought they were supposed to turn into.

As men and women flail around and about today, with silences and invisible question marks in the air between them, at least part of the fault can probably be traced back to that: to the days when we thought we had to be Hopalong Cassidy and June Cleaver. If we never managed to live up to it—well, no surprise.

Although when you are young there are certain times, if you are very lucky, when you meet people whom you really do hope you can grow up to emulate. At 50 you look back and it seems like a dream.

In the spring of my senior year in high school, a bunch of us went to Florida for vacation. One night a kid named Gary Herwald and I were walking around Miami Beach, and we went into the bottom level of one of the old hotels.

About twenty feet away, standing by himself and looking into the window of a shop, was a black man wearing a business suit. In Miami Beach in the middle of the 1960s, it was more than a little unusual to see a black person in one of those hotels, unless the person was an employee. Gary and I looked over, and we could hardly believe what we thought we were seeing.

So we walked over to the man, and Gary said the words: "Excuse me. Are you Dr. King?"

And the Reverend Martin Luther King Jr. said that yes, he was, and he shook our hands. He had just won the Nobel Peace Prize, and had been featured on the cover of *Time* magazine. He spoke graciously with us; we told him how much we admired him, and he asked us where we were from. When we said we lived in Ohio, he smiled and said, "I didn't think you boys were from Florida."

Whenever I see Gary now, we talk about that. It feels a little like having met Thomas Edison or Abraham Lincoln—like having stepped into a history textbook. But because it took place in our own lifetime, the history part really doesn't sink in. I think of all the future history books that will be written for students in the centuries to come, and of Dr. King's place in them. And I think of time passing by, the time in which a person has an opportunity to accomplish what he may during his years on Earth. I think of walking with Gary across the hotel floor to introduce ourselves to Dr. King, and I realize that on that day Martin Luther King, winner of the Nobel Prize, was 36 years old.

There are things that please you now. They are small pleasures, but lovely—going out for a pizza by yourself, shooting baskets on an outdoor court, drinking a beer from the can as you listen to a local band playing on the terrace behind a restaurant.

They are all a part of that dichotomy between being 50 and at the same time feeling much younger. And as you look ahead, you can't quite see yourself doing some of these things at 60. Not that you won't be able to—but you sense you won't want to. Walking to the local pizza place on a whim just to sit by yourself and have a small double-pep, well-done—as you're sitting in the booth now, having that pizza, it's as if you can at the same time see yourself on a screen, and you know that the picture is destined to change. The 60-year-old you won't be in this booth. The 60-year-old you is going to be different.

He won't be shooting the baskets—or so you think, as you launch a shot toward the rim. Of course, thirty years ago you never would have told yourself that you'd be doing this at 50. And, in fact, you don't do it all that often—but you're just about sure you won't do it at all at 60. As the band behind the restaurant plays, you know you won't be here at 60, either. Doesn't seem like it will happen.

This may be where some of the quickening inside of you comes from, some of the instinct to take in these small pleasures right now. At 60, you are afraid, these pleasures will not necessarily apply. Savor them today. You sense they bear an expiration date.

● ● ●

And then there are moments that stop you in time.

You're driving down the streets of a quiet neighborhood, and you see a kid in his driveway, bouncing a tennis ball off the sloped roof above his family's garage. That's all he's doing—standing there aiming the ball halfway up the roof, letting it bounce back toward him, running to position himself where he thinks the ball will rebound, catching it, then starting all over again.

The kid is you. You've never met him, but you know what he's thinking about, because you were once that kid. It was another town, and another driveway, but that was you, bouncing the ball off the roof and using the time to think about all the things that were going on in your life. It was one of the most peaceful parts of your days.

No one knew; no one was aware that you used that time on the driveway to think about things. You don't have a lot of privacy in your life when you are that young—your family is all over the house, there are always voices talking and television sets playing and phones ringing. You're too full of energy to just sit and ponder life—sitting still is not an option you often choose when you're that young.

But the driveway—you and the ball and the sloping roof—the driveway gave you the private time to try to figure out all the things going on around you. The symmetry and the rhythm and the steady sound of the ball bouncing off the roof, the solitude of being alone on the driveway, waiting for a ball to come back to you . . . it all combined to give you something you needed.

Now, no longer that kid, you drive down this quiet street and there is that other kid, aiming the ball at the roof, thinking his thoughts, and you wish you could have that back. You wish you could find a driveway somewhere with a garage that has that kind of roof, and you wish you could do this every day, whenever you need to: stand there and throw a ball toward a spot on the tiles, trying to figure things out as you wait by yourself for the ball to return. You'd like to have that again.

But you can't. You're 50, and you can't spend your time throwing a ball at a roof. What would people think? What would the neighbors say? You're 50, and that's not what a person of 50 is supposed to do. You drive on by.

10

The Hyatt Regency Shady Acres, and Other Marketing Strategies

The marketers of the world are beginning to aim their products at men and women who are 50. Sometimes it is done subtly, sometimes quite directly. Always it is done for the same reason the marketers have always sought us out as we have grown from children to where we find ourselves now: They want our money.

And as always, they'll get it.

The Pain Relief Wars, in case you haven't noticed, are no coincidence.

If you have observed that new formulations of pain relievers are hitting the shelves seemingly every week—if not every day—then you are correct. Suddenly, after years of the same old brands of pain relievers doing the job perfectly well, there are new over-the-counter pills being introduced to the public with the speed and fury that British Invasion record albums hit the racks in 1964.

Only now the brand names on the products aimed at us aren't Herman's Hermits or the Zombies—they're chemical-sounding appellations, encased in brightly colored packages with promises printed on the outside, promises of the quickest relief ever from the woes that are racking our heads, our backs, our ankles. The old pills aren't good enough for us, the pharmaceutical companies are telling us; look what's inside this box.

The marketers have discerned that no longer, at 50, are we necessarily seeking joy, or instant gratification. Surcease from hurt will do. The Pain Relief Wars are a growth market if ever there was one.

The Hyatts and Marriotts and their various competitors, if they have any brains, will begin to deemphasize opening more and more business hotels and resort properties, and shift their planning to a potentially far more lucrative area of the hospitality industry.

Which is retirement homes. Nursing homes, too, if you really want to get dismal about it.

The big hotel chains have for a long time made their money by making our lives on the road easier with fax machines, twenty-four-hour room service, free breakfasts on the concierge floors, and other pleasing amenities. That's how they won our loyalty—by making our business travel a little more pleasant. Now let's see them make the next step easy for us. It's coming up soon enough, although not right now, and it will be a more daunting challenge than the one they faced when we were merely business travelers—this coming challenge of making us smile as we are led away from our offices and homes and into the sunset. But if they can pull it off—if they can persuade us to gravitate toward their glowing logos, even when those logos are mounted atop senior citizens' communities—they'll make billions, and their stockholders will do cartwheels of joy.

The marketers assume they can still fool us.

Take a look, for example, at those new bags of potato chips—the ones with pictures of bottles of famous brands of barbecue sauce on the front.

For years, barbecue potato chips were generic and un-apologetic—the same fat-laden, calorie-heavy chips with a spicy red coating on them. They were bad for you but they tasted pretty good.

Now, though, there are the pictures of the famous bottles of barbecue sauce. As if the manufacturers expect us to believe that this is not your regular potato-chip-eating en-counter—this is a gourmet experience, high-class and so-phisticated and to be much appreciated.

And of course we go for it. We buy the bags of red-coated chips and scarf them down. Because that picture of the bottle on the outside of the bag does, in fact, make our mouths water. As they knew it would.

In the community of 50-year-olds, the phrases "good podia-trist" and "good dermatologist" have the same titillating ring as "king and queen of hearts of the Valentine's Day dance" did when we were 15.

You want an introduction. Those are people you wish you knew.

You notice people your age trying to make canes, crutches and knee braces look jaunty. They're being helped out by the people who manufacture those items.

So you see the canes decorated with floral patterns; the crutches with arm pads made of bright neon-colored foam rubber; the knee braces with pictures of Tweety Bird on them. This is a whole new market: people who at 50 want to give out the message, "I'm not decrepit, I'm just in the shop for repairs."

Not a bad message, by the way—not a bad way to approach your body being broken. The same way that orthopedic physicians now advertise themselves as being in "sports medicine," the cheerily designed braces and canes tell the world that their bearers are warriors knocked out of combat, not middle-aged men and women falling apart at the seams. Smiling all the way.

A worthy idea. And for the manufacturers' profit margins, it doesn't matter whether they're selling a Day-Glo cane or a plain wooden cane, as long as they do, indeed, sell a cane. The customer is always right. Give the lady what she wants.

An early-warning sign that you, at 50, are falling prey to the pitches that are being directed at you:

You're twenty seconds into a denture-adhesive commercial before you tell yourself: Wait a minute. Why am I paying attention to this? I don't even wear dentures.

Ah, but someone out there is counting on the fact that you probably will. If not you, then your neighbor. And you were sort of drawn into that little plotline in the commercial, where the guy bites hard into an apple and remains confident and happy, weren't you?

What Dick Clark on *American Bandstand* used to represent to you, the likable guy who stars in the syndicated corner-pharmacist feature on local TV news shows is about to become.

He stands there in his white pharmacist jacket, explaining in the friendliest tones what are the side effects of the

pill that's being featured today, and what this topical cream
can and can't do for you, and how long it takes these capsules to kick in once you swallow them. He's so *nice*—even if
you've never heard of the medicine he's talking about today, you never know when you may need it. And chances
are that tomorrow he'll be talking about something you
already have in your medicine cabinet.

The reason this guy is able to syndicate his feature to
local TV newscasts all over the country is that he's discussing things that the 50-year-old audience is starting to want
to know about. If anyone had asked you what kind of feature you'd like to see on your local news, you never would
have thought to mention this one—the idea of liking such a
thing would not have occurred to you. But once you see it,
you're hooked.

Especially when the guy talks about the new stuff—the
new prescriptions and lotions. Just like Dick Clark introduc-
ing you to the newly released records every week back in
1959, when the kids on *Bandstand* gave it a 95, because it
had a good beat and they could dance to it. The TV pharmacist holds up a new spansule, and you can just about
hear people of 50 all over the country giving it a 98—it's
easily swallowable, it reduces the inflammation, and you can
take it without upsetting your stomach. The pick-hit of the
week.

It strikes you one day that you still believe the top brands
you first learned about remain the top brands. Even if they
aren't.

You assume that Peter Pan peanut butter is the best-seller
in its field, as are Gant shirts and Pepsodent toothpaste and
Lavoris mouthwash. You take it for granted that more people chew Wrigley's Spearmint than any other brand of
chewing gum, that more people wear Penney Towncraft

T-shirts, that more people eat Kellogg's Corn Flakes for breakfast. You have absolutely no idea whether any of this is true, and you belatedly realize that this is why advertisers have always spent so much money trying to lure teenagers as customers, even though teenagers don't control their families' purse strings. The reason is that the brand loyalties a person develops early in his or her life tend to stick—and that if they can get you when you're young, they won't have to go to such lengths to try to lure your attention when you're older and set in your ways.

Not that it stops them. They're after you now, every day and in every way. But they wish they didn't have to be.

A subtle shift in how advertisers see us:

There's a commercial for some kind of ginseng powder, or a similar health product. A guy of about 50 is running on a scenic country road, and in voice-over he says that he's driven along this road in his automobile millions of times before, but never noticed how pretty it was until lately. He says that since he's started using this health-promoting product, things like appreciating the beauty of this roadway have opened up to him. The product, he says, was recommended to him by his daughter.

Which is the just-beneath-the-surface key to the commercial. Although we don't see the guy's daughter, we assume she is a young adult, probably in her 20s. And that she knows certain things about feeling healthy—and that her dad is grateful that she has shared this knowledge with him.

That's the shift, right there: the assumption that a generation younger than we are has knowledge of things we are unaware of—things that can help us. And that we accept the advice of those younger people, confident that their knowledge is probably right.

For the first time since we became consumers, we, at 50,

are being depicted as being somewhat needful. There will be more of this. It's just beginning to show up in advertising now, but as we grow older it will become a recurring theme. And we'll probably like it.

However, if the people who make TV commercials don't want to completely lose the generation turning 50, they'll stop moving the camera around.

This started with MTV—a herky-jerky camera motion, combined with the camera being turned at odd angles. Apparently this was supposed to give a cinema-verité feel, combined with an implicit rejection of the old camera-atop-the-steady-tripod way of doing business.

Only trouble is, it gives you a headache to watch it. And makes you nauseous. Maybe it works for viewers who are 13, but for anyone else it feels like you've been spun around twenty times and then asked to walk a straight line. On top of that, add the new quick-cut technique of editing the film so that there is a different image every quarter second, and instead of selling a product to the potential customers, the ad agencies are making those customers queasy.

You need a Dramamine to get through a single thirty-second commercial. Which might be all right if the product the advertising agency is trying to sell is Dramamine, but is counterproductive for any other kind of merchandise. Plus, there is no longer anything at all original about this. It's derivative and stale. Hold the camera still. We're not going anywhere—we just want to see the picture. And the product.

Marketing toward people who are 50 presents a challenge to advertisers and manufacturers that has nothing to do with the specific goods they are hoping to sell. Rather, it is an offshoot of the difference in the world of American business that the 50-year-old customers grew up in, and the world of business they find themselves in the middle of now.

The America of thirty-five and forty years ago—the business America that we first knew—was an America defined by the word "General." So many of the top companies, the ones our parents trusted, had that word in their titles. General Motors. General Electric. General Foods. General Mills. General Dynamics. The word spoke of an America that valued bigness, one-stop shopping, an all-encompassing corporate paternalism.

Somewhere along the way, this changed. The American business environment became a boutique culture—little subgroups of manufacturers and store categories, serving narrow consumer interests. Even if, in fact, the seemingly small manufacturers were owned by huge multinational corporations, the customer was not supposed to know it. General was out; tiny was in.

And now? The merchandisers—and the customers—have to decide which symbolism they want. There is something personal and inviting about the depiction of every business as being small and focused. But there was something reassuring about the culture of the General—the size and the solidness of it all. So which is it going to be? You can't very well have a company called General Muffins. Although it might be worth trying.

Not to dwell too long on the booming field of pills and medications for 50-year-olds.

But as long as there is such an outcry over the high price of prescription drugs, there's an obvious solution that should satisfy everyone.

The best way to lower the amount of money people have to pay for their prescriptions is to allow big corporations to sponsor the pills. Right there on the prescription label, taped to the bottle the pharmacist prepares: "Budweiser presents Flexeril (Take one tablet two times daily. May cause drowsiness.)." "Chevrolet presents Voltaren (Take one tablet two times daily, 15 minutes after eating.)." "Panasonic presents Vasotec (Take one tablet every morning as directed by physician.)."

Everyone wins. The advertisers reach the men and women of 50 and older in a way guaranteed to grab their attention (how are the advertisers supposed to spend their promotional money as they try to attract us—sponsor skateboard contests and beach parties?). The people of 50 and older pay much less money for their prescriptions, because the pharmaceutical companies' costs are knocked way down by the advertising dollars that are coming in. "American Airlines presents Claritin (Take one tablet daily.)." The full flower of capitalism at its most creative and cost-efficient.

P. T. Barnum couldn't, in his wildest dreams, have hoped for a bigger group of pushovers than the people who are turning 50. A sucker born every minute? He would have amended that phrase to make it every second, had he been around to meet the Skybox Generation.

The skyboxes and corporate suites in America's arenas and stadiums are the ideal symbol for what easy marks we are. The skyboxes—some of them selling for up to $400,000 (individual game tickets not included)—represent the spending ethic people have come to embrace and even eagerly pursue: handing over huge sums of money for something they are told will provide great pleasure, will provide happiness that was not present in their lives before. Not thinking about the fact that the game down on the field below is still the game they used to pay much less for, when they sat in a mere seat instead of in a skybox.

So the Skybox Generation eats catered meals and reclines in upholstered captain's chairs and is offered Baileys liqueur in milk-chocolate cups as the baseball players or the basketball players cavort on the distant fields and floors. And as the members of the Skybox Generation leave the arenas, they sometimes have on their faces the bewildered expressions of Barnum's carnivalgoers, departing the canvas tents with this nagging feeling that someone has picked their pockets—yet willing and eager to come back the next night and have it done to them all over again.

Yes, the American economy is a free market.

But at 50, you might want to resist the marketers who are attempting to sell you Rollerblades, tank tops and Game Boys.

The companies that produce lighthearted birthday cards get a little desperate in their humor when the numeral on the front of the card is "50."

The card manufacturers are evidently trying their hardest:

"You're very well preserved for 50." (Open the card.) "It must be the alcohol."

"Celebrate your 50th by making mad, passionate love." (Open the card.) "What the hell, you've got five minutes to spare, don't you?"

"You? 50? I can't believe it." (Open the card.) "You don't look a day over 70."

No harm done, though. Because the cardmakers' only alternative is something that would really depress the people who receive the cards:

To be serious.

•   •   •

The new merchandising toward the generation turning 50 even comes out of the ceilings above their heads.

I was in a public building during a business trip when I was stopped dead in my tracks by the sound of Muzak.

Now, a person isn't supposed to notice Muzak. The whole point of Muzak is that it's designed to be the ideal soothing piped-in background music. On this particular day, though, the Muzak stopped me as effectively as if it had been an electric prod.

For instead of a lushly orchestrated string arrangement from the score of *The Sound of Music* or *The King and I,* this was something else. The song I was hearing was, indeed, soft and bland and filled with strings, like all elevator music is designed to be.

But the song—I was almost sure of this—was "Double Shot (Of My Baby's Love)."

It was muted and it was gentle and it was all-instrumental Muzak—and it was "Double Shot (Of My Baby's Love)."

"Double Shot (Of My Baby's Love)," briefly popular in the summer of 1966, was a raucous, prototypical bar song recorded by a raucous, prototypical garage band known as the Swingin' Medallions. "Double Shot (Of My Baby's Love)" was the only hit the Swingin' Medallions ever had— and with good reason. There were only two things you could do while listening to "Double Shot (Of My Baby's Love)"—drink beer and throw up. That's what the song was made for.

And here it was. On Muzak. I looked up toward the ceiling. The orchestral strings were ever so sweetly playing the part of the song in which the Swingin' Medallions had sung: "It wasn't wine that I had too much of . . ."

I am a realist. I knew that instrumental versions of Beatles songs were now featured on Muzak. I knew that instrumental versions of Simon and Garfunkel songs were now featured on Muzak. The world changes.

But the Swingin' Medallions? "Double Shot (Of My Baby's Love)"?

I had to know. I called Muzak's world headquarters in Seattle. An executive named Bruce Funkhouser checked the Muzak computer, which keeps track of all songs played, and said, "Here it is. Yes, yes . . . we do feature that song. To be precise, it played last Wednesday afternoon at fifty-seven minutes and thirty-one seconds after five o'clock."

He told me that Muzak used to feature only songs like "It Might As Well Be Spring"—the kinds of songs performed by Mantovani or the Jackie Gleason Orchestra. But the company had expanded its repertoire. Muzak's goal, he said, was still "to soothe people and put their minds into a comfort zone." Thus, he said, every song on Muzak is specially arranged and recorded by Muzak's musicians. The lyrics are removed, the sound softened.

But, I said to Funkhouser, I always thought that the songs on Muzak were supposed to be the traditional tunes that middle-aged Americans remembered from deep in their pasts.

"Yes?" Funkhouser said.

And I understood. That's what "Double Shot (Of My Baby's Love)" has become—a traditional and nostalgic American tune, well suited for Muzak. That's what they're selling—and that's what the people who are turning 50 are buying.

Not that they still necessarily want to drink beer and throw up while they listen.

It would be sort of impolite, in an elevator.

• • •

One of the things you give up at 50 is the simple pleasure of reading a magazine and thinking that it is just a magazine.

You know better. You know that the real purpose of that magazine in your hands—whatever magazine it is—is to deliver you to advertisers. Just as certainly as the magazine is delivered by the postal carrier to your house, you, too, are being delivered—to the people who paid for all those four-color full-page ads.

There's nothing wrong with this—it's just the way things work. Network television also works that way—the reason the shows are there is to hand you to the advertisers. The people who run the places—the magazines, the networks—may very well take pride in the stories and shows that they put out. But that's not why the stories and shows are there. The stories and shows are there so that a certain number of living, breathing bodies, your body among them, can be guaranteed to the merchandisers who are buying the ad space and the commercial time.

At 50, you leaf through a new issue of your favorite magazine and you think about this. Before you've settled in to read a single story, the publishers have done their job. They have delivered you.

You were once happily unaware of this. Among many other facts of our national life.

"I was in the bathroom upstairs at my house, and I meant to take a book downstairs with me."

A friend was telling me this.

"When I got downstairs," he said, "the thing that bothered me was not that I forgot to take the book with me. The thing that bothered me was that I forgot what it was that I forgot to do."

Sound familiar? It's the reason behind a growing line of

products aimed at people turning 50. They're miniaturized electronic-reminder devices—little computer-chip-driven machines that you can stick in your pocket, speak into, and remind yourself what you're supposed to do. Like memo pads, but voice-operated.

They're not for great creative endeavors, or futuristic high-tech pursuits. Instead, they're a little like hip replacements—only they're memory replacements, or at least memory enhancers. Intended to tell you the things you never used to need telling.

"Like where you parked your car," my friend said.

Exactly. Difficult stuff like that.

Yet another truth of American marketing you'd just as soon, at 50, you didn't know:

The companies that make the food you buy in the grocery store pay money to the groceries for the right to have the food on the shelves.

At least a lot of them do. That's how, increasingly, the supermarket game is played. Not quite as romantic a notion as the idea that the food got there because the grocer thought it was good, and thought that you, the customer, might like to take it home to your family. Or even the unrealistic notion that food has a right to be on the grocery shelves because . . . well, because it's food. Where else is it going to be, if not on the grocery shelves?

Nowhere, apparently. So the asparagus pays through the nose. The pears ante up. It's a rough world out there. Even if you're a canned plum.

For some reason a picture of a palm tree—any palm tree, even the most sickly-looking palm tree—on a brochure or in an advertisement from a vacation locale is enough to get you excited every time.

Even if the picture of the palm tree isn't a photograph—
even if it's just a drawing of a palm tree. A *bad* drawing of a
palm tree. Palm trees are a guaranteed lure. They are for
you, they were for your mother and father before you, they
were for your grandparents before them. A palm tree, of all
things. Show you one, and you're on your way to the airport.

When the Beatles' anthologies albums were released in
1995 and 1996, the business pages of the newspapers ran
stories saying that the record companies (all right—CD
companies) had to come up with an inventive strategy for
distributing the albums to retailers. The challenge, according to the business-page reports, was to make sure that the
albums were sold in untraditional places like airports and
drugstores, because the target audience—the Americans
who are turning 50—don't go to record stores.

Interesting observation, and accurate. You're not sure
you want to know where else they've figured out that we no
longer go.

For all the money that beer and soft drink companies spend
to try to persuade us to buy their products, is there any
beverage they can make us believe tastes better than when
we used to stick our heads into the sink on a sultry summer
afternoon and gulp the cold water as it rushed straight
from the spigot? Can they match that feeling?

And is there any sight or sound they can put in the commercials that can top the sound of a glass soda pop bottle
clanking against the hard metal sides of those old machines
where you put the coin in and then, guiding your bottle by
its cap, worked it through the long, deep grooves until you
got it to the spot where you could pull it out, hearing the

click and then the clunk as the machine released it and let you have it?

To understand how the nation's merchandisers view us at 50, all you really have to do is consider the evolution of the way business hotels have tried to win our patronage and loyalty.

First there was Shampoo Wars. The general managers of hotels from one coast to the other apparently believed that whoever could pamper their guests by offering the most exotic, distinctive shampoos in hotel bathrooms—honey almond shampoo, mink oil shampoo, coconut shampoo—would own the travelers' hearts.

Then the battleground shifted to Mini-Bar Wars. General managers loaded up the little refrigerators in the rooms with every kind of alcohol and sweet they could cram in. Apparently the thought was that whichever hotel chain could devise the most opulent and hedonistic mini-bars would secure the lifelong devotion of the business traveler.

Several years later, though, there was a dramatic shift. Shampoo Wars and Mini-Bar Wars waned, to be replaced by Cookie Wars. Hotel general managers, evidently figuring out that what the business traveler really wanted was not garish decadence but rather a return to Mom, offered free cookies at night: chocolate chip cookies, oatmeal cookies, peanut butter cookies, often warm, occasionally accompanied by a glass of milk, for which increasingly weary travelers seemed surprisingly grateful.

Now—with so many business travelers reaching 50—there is a new front in these wars. On the nightstands of certain hotels, travelers can find small booklets filled with pleasant stories—a different set of stories for each night of the traveler's stay. The stories provided by the hotel chains, each story just long enough to lull a tired traveler to nod

off, are intended as a soothing and comforting touch before slumber. Thus, Bedtime Story Wars appears to be the
next frontier. At 50, the traveler is too exhausted for anything else. Here's your reward for a lifetime of work—a nice
little story for you before you turn the lights out.

11

You Guys Don't Belong at Urban Outfitters

The way you are starting to regard people who are younger than you tells you as much about yourself at 50 as it does about them:

The "you guys" tendency by young people working in service and hospitality professions is beginning to drive you crazy.

You see people of your own age or older sit down at a table in a restaurant. A waitress in her 20s approaches the table and brightly says, "Can I bring you guys a drink before dinner?"

You know this shouldn't annoy you. You know she is only trying to be friendly and welcoming. But you are 50 years old. You have never met this person. You are paying to be here. You are not "you guys."

Not that you ever say anything about it. You smile and

mumble your drink order. Waiting for the inevitable moment when she will come by again and pose the question:

"Are you guys ready to order yet? Or did you need a few
more minutes to study the menu?"

You will not drink out of one of those floppy foil bags that
younger people buy their fruit concoctions in. You also will
not drink out of a little juice box with a sharp plastic straw
stuck into it. Cups and glasses are just fine. A can will do.
There is no thirst that is severe enough to make you slurp
from a box.

You try not to make any critical comments to younger people in your family who do their shopping at Urban Outfit-
ters and Banana Republic and Old Navy Company and the
like. This compulsion of theirs to purchase their basic clothing needs at places intended to make them feel as if they
are in the midst of some sub-Saharan saga, or lost on a
safari . . . it's harmless enough. They should be able to do
it without being smirked at.

Yet you ask yourself what it is that has happened between
the time you were a kid and the time they are kids that
necessitates their lives being rigged up as a nonstop theme
park. You needed a shirt or a pair of socks, you went to
Sears or Montgomery Ward. These ones today, they need
some underwear, they go to a place designed and named
with the idea of making them feel like life in the city is as
full of peril and potential derring-do as an expedition
through the underbrush.

Come to think of it, they may be right.

The most popular television shows among young people—
the shows about groups of friends just out of college trying
to make it in the city, or about cute children with no par-

ents who are being raised by a harried and lovable older brother—are seen by tens of millions of people each week. More Americans know the characters and plotlines of those shows than know the storyline in *Gone with the Wind*.

You have no idea what those shows are. You have no idea who the characters or the actors are. You are aware they must be famous and beloved—their pictures are always popping up in the newspapers and magazines you read, accompanied by wry allusions to their on- and off-camera relationships with other members of the casts—but you are without even a hint of what all of this refers to. For all the intersection the problems of these characters have with your life, the shows might as well be appearing on a foreign-language channel. Devoted to the customs and conventions of, say, Pitcairn Island.

You do worry about what nostalgia is going to mean to these young people in the not-so-distant future.

You see two girls of about 15 talking. One has something she is looking at. It's her pager—the alphanumerical beeper her parents have given her to carry.

She is pushing a button on the pager and staring at its display screen. Her friend, exasperated with her, says:

"Oh, will you stop living in the past?"

The first girl had clicked her pager display back to a phone number she had stored when it came in a few weeks ago—apparently the phone number of a boy who had paged her. She is gazing at it with the love-smitten expression her grandmother may have had when she caressed a treasured and lacy Valentine.

"Get over it," her friend says.

The first girl continues to dreamily reminisce about the digits on her pager.

• • •

There is a strong case to be made that we who are 50 got better and more understandable advice and direction from our parents than children today are getting from theirs. Even if we didn't know it at the time.

At an amusement park I saw a young mother, apparently displeased with her 4-year-old son, say to him:

"Your attitude leaves a lot to be desired today. Chill out, OK? I want you to take a deep breath."

Thing is, she didn't seem to think she was sounding like a pop psychology book. Apparently she thought she sounded like a mom. And to the kid, who didn't know that parents ever sounded any other way, she undoubtedly *did* sound like a mom.

Although, at that moment, the distant remembered echo of "You're going straight to your room when we get home, young man" had the evocation and historical resonance of a vintage speech by Theodore Roosevelt.

Who carried a big stick, and seldom, by all accounts, chilled out.

If you take a look at movies from the 1940s, you will be struck by how differently teenagers—especially teenage boys—were depicted then, particularly in relation to their fathers.

The prototypical movie teenager in the years around World II was a gangly, awkward kid in a short-sleeved shirt, his voice squeaking as he passed through puberty, his pants high on his waist, his hair slicked goofily back like the cartoon guy on the Big Boy hamburger-stand sign. He was close to in awe of his dad—and if not in awe, at least deeply respectful of his dad's wealth of experience. "Jeepers, Dad, the fellows at school will flip when I show them your combat ribbons!"

Today's prototypical movie teenager is a smoldering cauldron of sex, attitude, and resentment—his dad's the dork, not him. If anyone has a squeaky voice and a short-sleeved shirt, it's the movie father. Whom the movie son, if he feels like it, will either kill or—if the movie dad's lucky—beat up.

To the strains of a soundtrack CD that will within three weeks of the movie's release be playing in a million suburban teenage bedrooms, and that will fill its teenage listeners with all the triumphant pride of "Victory at Sea."

Do you have any memory at all of knowing how much a baseball card was worth? Other than the nickel it cost to buy it and the slab of pink chewing gum that came with it?

Of course not. It was not something that ever occurred to you to think about. Not only did you not know what a baseball card was worth, you didn't know what *anything* was worth. The prices of things—at least anything past a Coke or a Hostess cupcake—were outside your field of enlightenment.

Today a 10-year-old knows how much his friend's parents' house cost. He knows how much every brand of computer costs. He knows far more than you do about how much different makes of automobiles cost—with or without options. When he looks at a baseball card, he doesn't even see the face of the ballplayer—all he can see is the price he'll be able to get for the card on the open market. You feel like you ought to toss him the financial section of the paper every morning, while you keep the sports section. Or the comics.

"Sir" and "ma'am," now that you're routinely hearing them from younger people, have a vaguely different sound than you'd expected they would.

When you say those words (the Elvis legacy again), they are meant as a token of respect, or at least of deference.

But when they're directed at you by those twenty and thirty years your junior—on the rare occasions when those people drop the "you guys" salutation—you sense that the words are intended as almost the opposite of respect. "Sir" and "ma'am," the way they're directed at you, are empty, popcorn-like words, words devoid of nutrition or meaning, said indifferently and with an implied yawn. "Yes, sir" (Yes, you harmless old fool, to whom I must be nice if I want to keep my job). "Yes, ma'am" (Yes, you generic human to whom I must speak on my way to quitting time).

"Sir" and "ma'am," it occurs to you once you have become sir and ma'am, are not goals to be particularly aspired to.

There are certain sentences you overhear young people saying, sentences you yourself may have said at one point in your life but cannot even imagine saying now.

Example:

"We made real good friends with the bartender."

This was spoken by some college students on spring break. The sentence was said with an undercurrent of unexpressed pride, the students summing up the meaning of the previous evening, away from home and family, their mothers' sons but not wanting to admit it, drawn toward an authority figure who knows the ropes and thus confers upon them some thirdhand sense of wizened experience, too. Like a required course in life that feels like an elective at the time: "We made real good friends with the bartender."

You did, too, long ago. Real good friends with about twenty thousand of them, if memory serves.

Also, not that it matters at this late stage of your existence, but when exactly did spring vacation become spring break?

• • •

Shock Theater was the name of the local late-night television show that was supposed to scare us silly on weekend midnights.

All it was was old movies like *Frankenstein* and *Mighty Joe Young*, shown with commercial breaks every fifteen minutes or so. To make the presentations even more scary, the TV station had a ghoulish host introduce the movies, but we could see that this was the same man who, in the afternoon, played Casper the Camel on the kids' cartoon show.

Nevertheless, it worked. We were obedient young souls; if adults had determined that we were supposed to be scared, then we would be scared. Many a Friday night sleepover erupted into screams and hollers at the grainy black-and-white sight of Boris Karloff emerging from one casket or another, to be interrupted several minutes later by a commercial from Lex Mayer's Chevrolet.

Makes you think about what it would take to shock today's young television viewers. Not only can they see graphic gore, total nudity, bloodshed and depravity and rage on their cable channels any night of the week, they also can watch their local newscasts to see realistic nonfiction footage of carnage and dismemberment and the worst of human cruelty.

Which is one more thing to ponder as we weigh the consequences of our new, censorless world: how the children who are growing up without censors will turn out now that their own *Shock Theater* is ceaseless and unrelenting and real.

Casper the Camel would weep.

And if children are being made older than they ought to be sooner than they ought to be in serious ways, it's happening in seemingly frivolous ways, too.

Witness the Boxer Shorts Generation—little kids of 6 and

8 who choose to get dressed in the morning in the same kind of garments their grandfathers did at 80. All they need to complete the picture is garters, knee-length socks, and a money clip.

When you were a kid looking in from the outside, the men's and women's locker rooms at the country club or swimming pool were forbidding places where the people spoke a secret language not intended for you.

At 50, you go into the locker room you've been going into for your entire adult life, and suddenly it's filled with people twenty and twenty-five years younger than you are. More and more it feels like a forbidding place where they speak a secret language, not intended for you.

A cover line on a magazine aimed at teenage girls:
    "How I Dealt with My Mom's Depression."
    You don't think we've screwed things up? You don't think we've taken our own problems out on the children, asking them to handle the things we adults haven't been able to? We can tell ourselves that this is honest and forthright and unblinking—not hiding the troubles of life, but bringing them out in the open for the children to see. There is a case to be made, though, that by doing away with the protective cocoon of childhood, by including the children in every agitation of adult life, we have failed them in ways we don't yet fully comprehend.

My mother's friend Henny Wolf was visited by her grandson. What happened next was a reassuring sign that we are not quite yet a monolithic nation—that what has overwhelming meaning to one enormous group of people is an utter question mark to another equally huge group.
    Henny Wolf took her grandson to a restaurant for lunch.

This was a place generally frequented by older men and women. There were a few teenagers in the restaurant, though, and their reaction to Henny's presence was confusing both to her and to the other senior citizens in the room.

The teenagers would repeatedly walk by Henny Wolf's table, smile invitingly at her grandson, giggle and squeal. He was a nice-looking kid, yes, but what was going on?

What was going on was that Henny's grandson—his name is Scott Wolf—had just gone on the air in a Fox television series called *Party of Five*. He was becoming the designated teenage hunk of the moment—the latest in a long line that started with Edd "Kookie" Byrnes and has wound through David Cassidy, Ricky Schroder, Luke Perry and others too numerous and fleeting to mention. Henny's grandson was a magnet to the young people who couldn't believe he was actually in this restaurant—and he was invisible to the people who did not watch *Party of Five*, who were not in *Party of Five*'s target teen audience, and who wouldn't know Scott Wolf from Scottie Pippen. Or Randolph Scott.

At 50, an instructive thing to keep in mind next time you're tempted to feel especially happy or especially sad about some turn of events in your career: Be assured that somewhere out there, nobody cares.

Would you, at 50, start smoking?

Of course not. Not if you never have. Which is why you realize that it goes without saying that the cigarette companies want to attract young people to their products. Why would they even go through the motions of protesting that they're not out to recruit young people? They're not going to persuade anyone who's already an adult to start—"Gee, I think I'd like to break the string of a lifetime without cigarettes today, and go out and buy a pack of Marlboros"—so there's only one place for them to turn. They may be able to honestly say they're not out to get the kids to start smoking today. Tomorrow will do. Or the day after.

The Deionization of America:

I saw a father in his early 30s throwing a peewee football to his son. The boy was young—maybe 5. The dad had to throw the football several times before the boy was able to clutch it to his chest.

"Touchdown!" the father yelled.

"Touchdown!" the mother, who was to the side watching, yelled.

And then the father said to the son:

"Did you do your dance?"

Kindly and gently and not as a joke. The child obediently started to prance around in an imaginary end zone, strutting and pointing his fingers and taunting an unseen opponent.

"Did you do your dance?"

Did you eat your vegetables?

Did you do your homework?

We're doomed.

The Sunday newspaper prints the full-page ad listing the dates of the summer concert series at the local outdoor amphitheater. You read it top to bottom. There's not a band on the whole list you can conceive of buying a ticket to see.

At 50 you should resist, if at all possible, the urge to try to figure out how to market things to younger people. Number one, it is none of your business. Number two, you will fail.

I was in Mansfield, Ohio, giving a speech at a local theater, and the editor of the daily newspaper invited me to meet with the staff before the evening event. One of the topics that came up—as it always does around newspaper offices these days, in a country where the act of reading sometimes feels like an endangered species—was the question of how to get younger people interested in reading their town's paper.

The ideas presented when this comes up in newspaper offices are always variations of the same suggestions. Run special sections for the "youth market." Try splashier graphics. Make the pictures bigger. Use more color. (In other words, make a newspaper like a TV screen—content aimed at the adolescent mind, big color pictures, words and design elements that jump out at you and make your eyes hurt.)

So in Mansfield, the staff was talking about how to make sure that the city's teenagers and young adults got in the newspaper-reading habit—how to persuade them to pick up the *Mansfield News Journal* every day—and they asked me for a suggestion and I came up with the only one I thought might work:

"Wrap each paper around a can of Budweiser before the paperboy tosses it at the front porch."

People like us have no idea how to market to young America. Which may be construed as something in our favor.

You know how you used to think it was funny that when you made cultural references to such things as *Gunsmoke* and Frankie Avalon, young people would look at you as if they had no idea what you were talking about? How it was amusing to find people to whom those kinds of references meant nothing?

The humor in it is going away. At 50, you are finding

more and more people who stare blankly when you mention these things—the joke's on you, not them. You might as well be talking about Rudy Vallee and Clara Bow.

Although this may be circling around again. With Nick at Nite and the fifties and sixties music revivals, we seem to be on the verge of once more doing something perfidious to the younger people: forcing our tastes and our performers on them. They know far more of our singers, actors, movies, and TV shows than we know of theirs. It's the ultimate mean joke we're pulling on them: We are forcing our nostalgia to be their nostalgia. We are making sure that when they get to be our age and look back on the entertainment that filled their world, it will be used entertainment that we chose for ourselves and then gave to them when we were through with it. Hand-me-down nostalgia.

Which brings us to the Rock and Roll Hall of Fame.

Putting our music in a museum may be sending an unfortunate signal to the world, not to mention to ourselves. As it is, the electric guitar—with all it represented about rebelliousness and noise and a cocky sense of cool—has become a visual symbol of our generation, the way the Model T was for our grandfathers'. Yet young people today still seem to need the electric guitar and use it. It's like mentally having to ask us to borrow the car every time they want to enjoy listening to a song. No wonder they seem a little upset with us all the time. Just wait until they fully figure out the Social Security numbers.

We may have had our faults. Many of them.

But as you walk the streets today, you look around you and think: At least our generation of mothers and fathers didn't wear roller skates and spandex tights as they pushed their babies along in their strollers. Walkman headsets, too.

• • •

Two men, around 25 years old, traveling sales representatives for a sporting-goods company, were having a drink after a day of sales meetings. They were talking.

"Ah, the territory's bad," the first man said. "You know—tennis is bad in the Midwest."

The second man said, "Yeah—and he's 46 years old."

Meaning this:

That the man they were talking about—the man not present—was considered, in their eyes, too old to have the hustle and drive to handle this territory, where the market for tennis equipment was considered difficult.

"The territory's bad." "He's 46."

They might as well have had the scalpels right out there on the table. They were carving his territory up, making plans on how to make it theirs. Using the language of business that was still new enough to them that it gave them a little burst of control and power just to speak it.

The next time they saw their 46-year-old colleague, they would undoubtedly give him a big smile. That's who's down there just beneath us—fellows like those two. Meaning no harm, nothing personal. Just preparing for a little business-style surgery.

A boy falls down on his bike, hurting himself. Crying, he runs toward his house.

A woman who lives in one of the houses by which he runs sees him, and tries to stop him to ask him what's the matter. She wants to help.

But now he is really terrified. This is the thing he has been taught to be most afraid of—someone he doesn't know coming up to him. His crying increases and he sprints away from the woman.

One more thing that today's children have had to learn:

the redefinition of what an adult is. The assumption that
any adult they don't know may be out to harm them. Nice
legacy we're leaving.

Your bosses are getting younger. You find yourself thinking
about what they were doing during various crisis points in
your career. For example: You figure out that on the day
you were requesting, and being turned down for, an opening in the company that would have meant a big raise, your
new boss was in the sixth grade.

As disorienting as that is for you to think about, it is even
more peculiar to try to figure out what your new young
bosses are thinking when they see you. If you try to see
yourself through their eyes, it may upset you. You think
about them going through your personnel file, looking at
your past evaluations and your salary history. Evaluations
and salaries that you were earning when they were still in
junior high school. *You* have never even seen your personnel file, and now it's an open book to them.

You think about whether you're making too much of this.
Even the ritual of saying "Good morning" to them takes on
a certain edge.

Among the words you never want to hear:
"Retraining."

Younger employees patronizingly promising to teach you
new skills, because the ones you have always had, the talents
of your lifetime, are no longer needed. Retraining. As if
you're a dog.

Where do you think they got the line about teaching new
tricks?

You see people in their teens and 20s wearing tour
T-shirts—the shirts sold by bands at their concerts, with the

lists of the cities and dates where the bands are playing this year printed on the back.

You try to envision what a tour shirt of your life would look like. All the dates, all the places, all the stops you've made. You've been on this tour forever; the tail of the shirt would reach to the bottom of the Grand Canyon, and even then there would be more shirt to go. And you've always been your own road manager.

Somewhere in the world, right now, a girl is deciding she would like to be a synchronized swimmer. Somewhere a boy is deciding to go into the Army. Somewhere a child is deciding to study to be a doctor.

All these decisions being made by young people today, this minute, will, by the time they are 50, define everything. The decisions being made right now will change their lives—the decisions will be refined and put into focus and what today seems like dreams to the people who are doing the dreaming will settle and solidify and become no-U-turns-allowed tunnels. Not today, though. Today the dreams are still allowed to be dreams—promises.

Be grateful for good timing:

At least you, at 50, missed the tattoo fad. You see all the young men and women with their big tattoos, and you think about what this is going to look like when they, and their skin, get to be your age.

You try to imagine Dennis Rodman at 70.

12

Life's Unanswered Questions: Toasters, Coleslaw, Davy Crockett

There may have been a time during your life when you assumed that, by 50, you would have all the answers. You now know that not only are you still looking for the answers, but that there seem to be more questions than ever.

Three-way lightbulbs, to name just one example. You have been told that as a citizen of our times you are supposed to familiarize yourself with the techniques and technology of the burgeoning worldwide computer network, but before you get started on that you wish someone would finally explain to you how those lightbulbs with three brightness settings work. What's the rule on changing them? If one setting burns out before the other two, do you toss the bulb out? Or are you supposed to wait until all three brightnesses have gone dim? Half a century into your life, you still don't know.

. . .

Shoes, too. In a shoe store I saw a man of about 50 trying on two different pairs of dress shoes. He was discussing the fit with the clerk. Then he turned to two women shoppers who were in the store and said:

"Excuse me. I have a stupid question. Is it better to get these a little too small, and let them stretch? Or a little too big, so they're not too tight?"

"Why not get a size that's just right?" one of the women said.

"They're never just right," the man said and the second woman said, in unison.

The first woman thought and said: "A little too small, so they don't flop."

The second women thought and said: "A little too big, so they don't pinch."

They didn't know any better than the man did. Why should they have? They were 50 years old, too. Still waiting for the day when they are old enough to have the answers.

At carnivals and county fairs when you were a kid, there was always a booth with a sign that said "See Yourself as Others See You."

There was some sort of double mirror behind the curtains. That phrase remains one of the most puzzling, slightly frightening thoughts there is. See yourself as others see you? You still sense that you don't know how others truly do see you—and like the kid who walked past the carnival booth without going inside, you're not sure you really want to know the answer to that one.

Forget finding world peace and the root of all happiness.

At 50, you're still looking for the ideal toaster.

•   •   •

All the millions of dollars spent on commissioning new scripts and plot concepts for movies, all the time and energy spent on creating the most spectacular and flamboyant special effects to put up there on the screen.

And at 50 you know that nothing they can ever come up with will outdo the emotion and impact of that little boy running after Alan Ladd in the final scene of *Shane*.

You know that professional wrestling is fake. You knew it back in the days of Argentina Rocca and Buddy "Nature Boy" Rogers, and you know it now as you zap past the World Wrestling Federation matches on the cable channels.

What you don't know is this:

The results, they can determine in advance. That part they can fake. But how do those guys manage to get thrown off the top ropes and onto their backs—and then get up again? How do those guys lie on the mat and have a three-hundred-pound opponent leap into the air and come down on them—and walk away from it?

They can't fake that. When you were 12, your buddies used to tell you that it was all done by the wrestlers banging their feet on the mat—that the loud banging of the booted feet made it seem as if the landings were harsher than they really were. But that doesn't explain it. You watch as a wrestler is picked up and slammed onto his back three times in a row. Then—struggling to get up from your chair without your own 50-year-old back cramping up on you again—you try to figure out how it's done.

In 1973, a year during which you were an adult, you could get a decent motel room for $12, and a good big-city hotel room for $32. You could get a steak for $6.95.

Today, in the big cities, a good hotel room—a single

room—can cost you over $200. A steak in a good restaurant can cost you $20.

You know all about inflation. That's not the question you have. The question is this:

If, from 1973 to right now, that hotel room went from $32 to $200, then what happened between 1776 and 1973? If it took less than twenty-five years for a hotel room to go up $168 in price, then why, in the first two centuries of U.S. history, did the price go up only $32? The steaks, too—if they more than doubled in price, going up by $13, in the last twenty-five years, then why did it take those two full centuries for them to go from zero to $6.95?

You think someone is pulling a fast one. But you can't spend too much time thinking about this; it's checkout hour, and they're adding state sales tax and a city occupancy tax surcharge to your bill.

All the shelves full of books giving advice about how to reach the top in the business world, all of the books telling people how to succeed in their personal relationships, yet the biggest challenge of all—both in business life and in personal life—is unchanged from what it has always been.

It's the challenge of getting someone interested who's not interested at all. If you could figure that out, you'd have the answer to everything. But no one ever really has.

What would happen if we decided today—right now—that we wanted to put an American on the moon?

We couldn't do it. If we had to go to the moon today, it could not be done. Something that the United States was able to do in 1969 is now beyond our capacity. So why did we go in the first place?

There used to be a joke about and among astronauts. Why did they go to the moon? So that they could meet women when they got back home. That's probably a more satisfying answer than the real answer—which seems to be, "We don't know." At 50, our long-vanished conquest of space serves as a minor parable for other things in our lives. We did something great, something that seemed impossible before we got it done. But if we were asked to do it now, we couldn't.

"Parental Guidance Suggested."

At 50, you see that advisory notice on movie ads, and you realize that you will soon be past the age where you need to make those decisions and provide that guidance any longer. You also realize that, every time in your adult life you saw the parental guidance sticker, you didn't think it was actually talking about you. "Me? Guide someone? I'm the one who could use the guidance." And now you're about to outgrow it, without ever having truly figured it out.

I know a person who, in his house, has twin curving grand staircases.

Like in an old movie about wealth and extravagance— staircases that wind down from the second floor to the first, staircases built for Olivia de Havilland to make a breathtaking entrance.

Every time I see my friend's staircases, I ask myself how he does it. Even if you're 50 years old, how do you walk down those stairs every morning, and what goes on in your head as you do it?

Probably nothing, at least in his case. He walks down in his robe and opens the door to bring the newspaper inside. His wife is already in the kitchen, making coffee. When he was 15 he had to decide which pair of shorts to wear on a summer day. Now, at 50, his daily decisions include which branch of his staircase to walk down in the morning. Evidently you can get used to anything.

This is what Fess Parker told me, once he had passed 50:

"Mr. Disney sent me on a tour of forty-five cities to promote the shows. I remember arriving at the airport in New Orleans. For twenty-five miles the route was lined with cars, people waiting to see me. They said it was a bigger reception than Eisenhower got when he was there. I grew accustomed to things like that. In Scotland, people pushed through the glass in a department store window. In Holland, they chased me down the street. There is nothing that prepares a man for something like that.

"When I started to do that job, I had never had a filling in any of my teeth. Within three years, I had thirteen. I think it must have been the tension. I was pulled off the set once, because there was some sort of Walt Disney Night at the Hollywood Bowl. They drove me to the Bowl, and they put me onstage in my Davy Crockett cap and uniform, and they handed me a guitar. The Los Angeles Symphony Orchestra was behind me, and the Roger Wagner Chorale, and I was supposed to sing 'Farewell to the Mountain.' There were twenty-five thousand people in the audience.

"It wasn't fun. It was awesome, but it wasn't fun. It had gone beyond the dream. I wasn't allowed to go out and eat. I was kept practically like an animal in my room. . . .

"There probably isn't a day when I don't get some reminder of what happened to me. When people find out who I am, they tell me how much I meant to them when they were children. But then there's the other side of it. I'll call some businessman, and I'll try to leave a message with his 21-year-old secretary, and she'll say, 'Wes Parker? How do you spell that?' "

It's sort of a reassuring thought: If the person you grew

up assuming had all the answers stored somewhere inside him—the person who was Davy Crockett—admits to that kind of turmoil and confusion, admits to not having the answers at all, then maybe it really is universal. If the King of the Wild Frontier confesses to at times having felt lost, then he's still sending us all a message, now that we're 50 and not 5. And it's probably just as well that he didn't let us know about all of this back then.

At 50 the words that still set your nerves on edge are: "Now, tell us *all about it.*"

The words are never spoken with bad intentions; they are meant as a sign of affection, of being interested in you. When you return from a trip, or from an important business appointment, or from a meeting you'd been planning for weeks, the people you are closest to want to know everything that has happened, before you are two steps in the door.

Today, as when you were much younger, your instinct is that right now you don't want to tell all about it. In fact, you don't want to tell anything about it. You want to decompress. You want to exhale. You want to do anything but tell anyone all about it.

The idea of telling all about it, while you're still walking through that doorway, is more wearying than whatever it is you have just gone through. You think about the World War II soldiers, and what must have gone on in their minds. Five years overseas, their duffels slung over their shoulders, home at last. And before they can put the bag down: "Now, we want you to tell us all about it. Don't leave out a thing."

Must have made some of them want to turn right around and head back to Italy or France. Where no one spoke their language.

• • •

Kids still do it—struggle to get a kite up.

You see it all the time, and as you watch the child trying and failing, as you see him let the wind catch the kite only to have it fall to the ground seconds later, see him untangle the string and run as fast as he can, the kite skittering along behind him, until he realizes that this isn't working, the kite isn't going anywhere . . .

As you see this, you have the urge to kindly tell him that he's never going to figure it out, and that the reason you know this is that you're 50 and *you* still haven't figured it out. He's not going to come up with the way to get this kite-flying thing right, because after all your years of trying you still don't have the secret to getting it right, and neither does anyone else you know.

You feel like saying that, but you don't say a word. It's better that he tries and finds out for himself.

(And when he gets home, the first words he hears will be: "Now, tell us all about it . . .")

At 50 you realize that the history books of the future will contain long entries on the person who invented the main-frame computer, the person who devised the atomic bomb.

You are beginning to understand that the men and women who really affected history—the men and women who made your life a little happier—never get their names in the history books, although they should.

For a good example: Who invented coleslaw?

You have no idea, but if there were any justice in the world, that person would not only be memorialized in history books, but would be the subject of exhaustive and celebratory biographies. Tell the truth: What development of mankind has made you feel better, fifty years on—a disk of software or a dish of coleslaw?

• • •

One feeling has changed not at all:

The feeling of walking into a party. Those first thirty or
forty seconds, when the people at the party are checking
you out, and you are checking them out—for all that has
happened in your life, the feeling at 50 of those first moments at a party is just about the same as when you were
first walking into parties in junior high school.

Even if you don't like going to parties anymore, those
first thirty seconds still have that feeling.

Come to think of it, maybe that's the reason you don't
like going to parties anymore.

It seems that the government's warnings to the public used
to pretty much be limited to "Don't Be a Litterbug" and
"Only You Can Prevent Forest Fires."

Today it seems that the government's attempts to warn
the public against the various and many perils of the world
are ubiquitous and endless—and, by all front-page evidence, fruitless. We're being warned more, about more bad
things, and getting decreasing results. The point of no return may have been reached when Smokey the Bear faded
into memory, to be replaced by security guards standing
next to airport metal detectors.

At 50, there are days when it seems that you are the person
responsible for everyone close to you who is older than you,
and also for everyone close to you who is younger than you.
And that no one is responsible for you.

It makes sense, at this time in your life. But you ask yourself whether anyone is ever truly ready for this—for being
the bearer of this responsibility, while knowing there's not a
person in the world who feels this responsibility toward you.
You'd say that it can be a lonely feeling, but you don't say

that. You don't want to worry the people who would hear you say it—the people for whom you are responsible.

Which way is better?

When you're 50, you miss the bustle and excitement and noise of the workplace when your job was new to you, and every moment of the day seemed to be potentially eventful.

Yet you resent it when a sudden sound interrupts your concentration in your office.

You want them both, at 50—the clamor and the silence. Either that, or you want neither.

Those people, people your own age, who appear to know the wine—do they, or are they only pretending?

You see them take a sip, perhaps sniff the air above the glass, then give a knowing nod to the waiter standing above them, giving the waiter the go-ahead to pour for the table.

What are they tasting that lets them know the wine is OK? What are they smelling? You have a suspicion they have no idea—that they're acting. And if they do know what they're doing, who taught them? Where did they learn this? No one ever taught you, so who taught them?

You see them, across the room, sipping and sniffing and solemnly nodding. You wish you could hook them up to a lie detector.

For your entire life, newspaper people in Washington have been writing long stories about appropriations bills moving through Congress.

And in your entire life, you have never read one of those stories all the way to the bottom. You most likely never will. You ask yourself whether anyone has. Yet even now, a whole new generation of journalism students is graduating, get-

ting ready to write another half century of appropriations-
bill stories.

Now if some enterprising Washington correspondent
would write a story explaining how the perfect bowl of coleslaw is made . . .

You begin to notice, at 50, how technological achievement
has far outdistanced human achievement.

From anywhere in the world, television producers and
technicians can provide a live picture of newsmakers changing the course of history during an event unfolding at that
very moment. No matter how remote the news event, the
networks are able to get the shot, shoot the picture and
sound up to a satellite circling the globe, bounce the images back down to an Earth station in the United States,
and put all of this on a screen in your home, in a fraction of
an instant.

And also on your screen, superimposed, will be the name
of the newsmaker—misspelled.

We can deliver the sights and sounds out of the stratosphere. Getting the names right, though, seems to be beyond us.

It's not so much a case of "be careful what you dream of,
because you just might get it"—it's more like, don't spend
too much energy on your most outlandish fantasies, because soon enough they'll be mundane and commonplace.

Hugh Hefner once luxuriated in being able to see movies
anytime he wanted—he had a full-time projectionist on his
staff, he had a storeroom full of movies in metal canisters at
the Playboy Mansion, he had a full-sized pull-down motion
picture screen—if he wanted to see *To Have and Have Not* at
midnight, he could see *To Have and Have Not* at midnight.
That's what being Hugh Hefner meant.

Now anyone living in a basement studio apartment with a VCR attached to the TV set and a video store in the neighborhood can do the same thing. One of the symbols of the power of the White House was that the president of the United States could make a phone call to anywhere in the world from anyplace he happened to be—even if he was high above America inside Air Force One. Now any grain-futures trader on his way back from vacation can slip his credit card into the seatback phone and, over his airline lunch, do the same thing.

You think back to when you were a kid, and you would hear about 50-year-old men—friends of your parents—who would "play the market." It sounded so rakish—they would gather at a stock brokerage office downtown, and watch the quotations move across an electric ticker board. To the outside world—and perhaps to themselves—they seemed to have the secrets of the financial milieu down cold. Sitting there watching the numbers, they appeared to be the in crowd of money, members of a private and exclusive club.

Today you are the 50-year-old, and there is no need for anyone to gather at a stockbroker's office. Anyone who cares can watch the stock quotations move all day long across the bottom of any cable television screen. You don't need, or even particularly want, company as you do this; you can do it in a hotel room on the road, you can do it in your office while you're working on something else.

The 50-year-old men of the past who used to sit together in the brokers' offices could assure each other that their positions in the market—and, by inference, their positions in life—were correct and savvy. Even if they knew that was not necessarily the truth.

Now, with the new disconnectedness, there's no such reassurance. The 50-year-old sitting alone in front of his TV set watches the numbers move across, and there's no one in the room to tell him that he's right.

Occasionally when you go into a public building and you notice that there are no security guards visible, you find yourself thinking: Who's watching this place?

Which is another aspect of the changed world you walk through at 50. Thirty years ago, if you had seen security guards posted in a public building, you would have guessed something was wrong. What are the cops doing here? Has there been a crime? Different America. Different assumptions.

The phrase "Play the cards you're dealt" never applies more than to a business executive who at 50 is appointed CEO, and looks around at the people who are suddenly all working for him.

High on the list of all the things you still don't understand at 50 is why anyone—audience, record company or fellow band members—would ever encourage a drum solo.

One of the ironclad lessons that every generation has taught to the next is: Learn a skill and stick with it.

Then, in the laptop era, you see a 50-year-old typewriter repairman.

One thing to make you content at 50 is the knowledge that no one has probably ended up exactly where he or she wanted to be.

Except for the president. And he's depressed.

An aspect of corporate life that was supposed to get better during the years since you started working is that the cold

"Personnel" department has been transformed into the warm "Human Resources" division.

So why is it that Human Resources seems even more impersonal, frigid and forbidding than Personnel ever did?

You can now buy a watch that works just about perfectly for $3.

And you still have no better idea than you did at age 6 of how this astonishing—all right, impossible—thing happens: A watch tells you what time it is. And is correct.

You would not want to count up, at 50, the number of nights in your life you have gone to bed angry about something.

Ours may be the last generation that will remember a time when high school athletes, when they enrolled in a university, talked about "going to college" instead of "joining a program."

Somewhere in the back of your mind, you realize that in terms of your business career these are supposed to be the power years. You look in the mirror, searching for someone powerful.

I heard a man in a restaurant saying to his wife, "If I ever have to go to the electric chair, I'd like lima beans and fried bratwurst for my last meal."

Which is a sign of how bad, at 50, is the sense of resignation over how life works:

You actually envy condemned men, because you sense that a convicted killer is the one person who is sure to be given exactly the food he wants.

• • •

A rather jarring thought that kicks in at 50 is that no one may be in charge, after all.

For most of your life you have looked at all of the craziness around you in the world, the turmoil and the disorder and the falling apart at the seams of the details of daily life, and you have presumed that there was someone who was supposed to take charge and straighten things out.

And then you are struck by the suspicion that no one really is. The big stuff—wars, revolutions, earthquake preparedness—yes. But the constant and growing insanities of everyday life . . .

The mayor's not in charge. The president's not in charge. The army's not in charge. So who is?

No one? Is that possible?

There are certain things you would think you have learned for certain by the time you're 50.

For example: You would think that, after five decades of living, you would know to have an extra pair of shoelaces around the house. Shoelaces do not break on schedule; they do not wear out on a predetermined day. Shoelaces—every pair of them—are eventually going to snap, and you are not going to know when this will happen.

So obviously you want to have an extra pair in the house. Obviously it will save you time and aggravation to have that pair in a drawer. You don't want to wait until your shoelaces break, and have to go out and buy new ones.

You do not have an extra pair of shoelaces in the house.

You have never had an extra pair of shoelaces in the house.

13

The Road to Happiness Is Paved with Dubble Bubble

When you look for fun and satisfaction at 50, the pursuit can lead you in directions you would previously never have supposed:

To feel the best payoffs of travel, you don't need to go on a lengthy voyage. You can put yourself in a thirty-second time machine rather easily: Pop a square of Fleer's Dubble Bubble or Bazooka into your mouth, chew it for half a minute, then spit it out if you want. The taste will already have taken you back to a place you loved. It'll do more for you than a weekend vacation.

That's because the spurs to the most enticing of sensations were programmed into you early. The tired, happy feeling of hurrying home just before dusk after playing four hours of baseball on the dirt diamond behind the junior high school; the bittersweet twinges of the last afternoon of summer; the walk from warmth toward cool evening in the beginning weeks of fall . . . the specific events that bring on those same feelings today are different from what first taught you the feelings, but your responses are unchanged.

The smell of motorboat gasoline outside a bait shop next to the water is an aphrodisiac that has nothing to do with sex. At 50 you smell that gasoline on the water, and for whatever reason over all the years it makes you want to sit on the dock with your shoes off and have a cheeseburger and a Nehi soda.

The Corpus Christi Rule of Travel is as true for you at 50 as it has always been:

Spending time in Corpus Christi with someone you like is better than being in Paris with people you don't.

On a Saturday afternoon you're bored, and you find yourself looking on a newsstand rack for the latest issue of *Popular Mechanics* or *Mechanics Illustrated*.

You haven't read either of those publications since you were 10 years old, when they seemed more than a little adult and cryptic and thrilling, with all their cutaway diagrams and blueprints and arcane specifications. You have absolutely no idea why you're looking for the magazines now. But before you even find them, the anticipatory kick has somehow returned.

The words "Girls, Girls, Girls" or "All Nude" on a building sign are nowhere near as enticing or filled with thoughts of forbidden pleasures as another word winking at you from storefront windows:

"Bakery."

• • •

More than just about anything else, the thing you value most at 50 is finding someone who means something when he or she says it.

It can be the smallest thing—in fact, it ought to be the smallest thing. "Good morning." "How are you?" People who aren't saying it because it's part of business, but because they really do mean it. About you.

All the stand-up comedy shows all over cable television, all the comedians with backwards baseball caps, curse words and jeans . . . all the barking from hyperkinetic audiences, all the loud and rapid-fire comedic vulgarity . . .

And all of a sudden, out of nowhere, you get this irresistible urge to watch Alan King.

Alan King, in a suit, telling jokes.

Where did *this* come from? You never even liked Alan King—or at least you never went out of your way to find him. So maybe it's not really Alan King you're in the mood to listen to, maybe it's the idea of Alan King.

Or is it really your father you're in the mood to listen to? Same thing, actually.

When you go on vacation, it takes you at least two or three days to get into the vacation mode—to slow down, to stop looking at your watch, to resist reaching for the phone every few seconds.

But when you return home, it takes you only two or three minutes to get back into the work mode. For some reason, at 50, enjoying yourself is often a harder task than working.

You are beginning to discover why older people like radio so much.

The sound of a ball game after dark, the announcer's descriptive phrases and the ebbing murmur of the crowd, the ball you can't see slapping into a glove you can't see, the harsh knock of the bat informing you of a well-hit pitch half an instant before the play-by-play man does . . .

The voice of one person on a late-night broadcast quietly speaking to you while the lights are out, offering the illusion that you are not part of a vast audience, but one person also, the only listener the voice coming out of your radio cares to talk to . . .

This is what radio has always been to older people. You don't buy into every one of the radio illusions just yet, but perhaps those older people have never bought all of it, either. Just enough to please and soothe them. At 50, you are listening to radio in a new way. Their way.

There are jobs that deliver services to people, and then there are jobs that deliver services to people.

I was walking along a street and a guy drove by in a truck with the words "Lance Snacks" painted on the side panels.

It had never occurred to me that Lance Snacks had their own trucks. Lance Snacks—the peanut butter crackers, the chocolate cookies, the stuff in cellophane wrapping that has been part of the semivisible backdrop in every non-haughty food place you can ever remember—Lance Snacks have always been sort of just *there*. Piled into big glass jars on the counter, stuck into metal clips on the display trees designed to show them off vertically—Lance Snacks are like air: atmospheric.

So here was the driver in the Lance Snacks truck (the letters in *Lance* painted in varying bright colors). Not a bad job to have, in the scheme of things—driving a Lance Snacks truck. Making people feel good, even while giving them something they know they probably shouldn't have. Which makes them want it all the more.

• • •

The late Earl Warren, chief justice of the United States Supreme Court, was once asked about his reading habits. "I always turn to the sports pages first," he said. "The sports pages record people's accomplishments, the front page nothing but man's failures."

At 50, you understand what he meant, because it has come true for you, too. It's not that you like sports any more today than you ever did—you certainly liked sports much more when you were a kid. But you're reading the sports pages more thoroughly than you read any other part of the newspaper, because you, like Earl Warren, feel the need to escape from man's failures and flaws rather than dwell on them.

Unfortunately, you are finding, the sports pages of Earl Warren's America are not the sports pages of today's America. Whatever evidence of weakness, greed and human frailty is found on the front page and business pages every day, it is often matched by what is on the sports pages.

But you persevere.

As best you can tell, the box scores are still unsullied.

The private electricity of music is part of the entertainment industry's marketing strategy today.

Millions upon millions of dollars are spent advertising tape and CD players that will pipe the music directly into the listener's ears with the intention of no one else hearing. It has become the rule rather than the exception: You choose the music, you plug the earphones in, and you alone receive it and enjoy it.

People who are 50 can only grin at this development. The great jolt of music first came to us precisely because it could *not* be private—and because we yearned to make it so. The tension inherent in that—us, wanting to listen alone, using record players that made solitude all but impossible—

opened up the illicit romance with our music that has defined our relationship with it for the last forty years.

The locked bedroom door, the sounds of the first 45 rpm
records we ever owned—"Party Doll" by Buddy Knox, "Rip
It Up" by Little Richard, "Singin' the Blues" by Guy Mitch-
ell, "School Days" by Chuck Berry—and the excitement of
listening to them behind that closed door, interrupted by a
parental banging, telling us to turn it off . . .

The merchandisers sell privacy right along with the music
today; you can hear whatever you want, and no one else will
know. It's not the same as that delicious feeling: the parental knocking stops, the footsteps walk away, you turn the
volume knob to a lower setting than before, and put the
needle on the swiftly spinning record one more time . . .

*All I want is Party Doll, to be with me when I'm feelin'
wild . . .*

Of all the luxuries life can offer at 50, few are as satisfying as
the knowledge you're going to have a parking space when
you get there. Guaranteed. No need to even think about it.

Pleasure? At 50?

You hate to admit it, but the meal you used to laugh at
Richard Nixon for liking—cottage cheese and catsup—
makes your mouth sort of water when you think about it. It
doesn't sound like such a bad combination at all.

Maybe with a little steak sauce for zip.

You've got to take your fun where you can.

There are certain things you once did for pleasure without giving it a second thought—a somersault, for example—that today is almost impossible to imagine yourself doing. If not for physical reasons, then for reasons of dignity.

It would be totally undignified for you, at 50, to do a somersault.

You realize that you have entirely too much dignity in
your life.

And you find yourself wanting to know when, exactly, soda
fountains in drugstores became financially inefficient.

They must have been highly efficient when you were a
kid—why else would there have been a fully staffed soda
fountain in every drugstore you ever remember? They
brought the customers in: People would stop by to have a
chocolate milkshake or a grilled cheese sandwich or a
cherry Coke, and while they were in the store they'd usually
end up buying something else, even if it was only a bottle of
Elmer's Glue. The marble counter, the stools with the red
revolving cushions that were beginning to fall apart (stuff-
ing sticking up through slits in the fabric), the long mirror
behind the fountain, the metal shake canisters ready to be
slid beneath the mixer . . .

At 50, you wish someone could explain to you why the
fountains would be so cost-inefficient today. Because you'd
love to be sitting at one right now, reading the paper and
sipping a malt.

You can give yourself small gifts that will resonate for years.

One suggestion:

Buy a ticket for a bedroom compartment in a railroad
car. You don't have to go far—an Amtrak trip to the next
state will suffice. Sit there in that bedroom, have the atten-
dant bring you a steak and a bottle of beer, gaze out the
window at America's ever-changing back yard, and take
your pleasures where you find them.

•   •   •

The best sleeping potion, you have learned at 50, is having completed a task.

For whatever reason, if there's something you need to get done, you know you'll sleep much better if you do it before you go to bed. Leaving it until morning will make you restless in the night. Finishing it now lets you sleep like a kitten.

At 50 the people in your life you value the most are not the ones who promise they can make you rich; not the ones who promise they can make you powerful; not the ones who promise they can make your existence easy.

The people in your life you value the most are the ones who can make you laugh. If you're lucky, they're still the ones who could make you laugh when you were 17. They're the friends you want around you all the time.

Like clockwork, when you're 50 black pepper starts to seem like an enticing spicer-upper to you. And spicy mustard begins to have a certain feel of raciness. It occurs to you that it is taking less and less to heat up your life a little bit.

A friend you knew from high school gets engaged again. This will be his third marriage. You receive a wedding invitation in the mail. You're happy for him.

And then you think:

He's 50 years old. Is being happy really the proper response to the news that he's going to try this one more time—at 50?

You decide that yes, it probably is. Maybe there's more of a reason to be happy for him now than when he was 22 and engaged. Back then, you were happy for him like you're happy for a football team that's easily running up the score in the first quarter. This time it's like you're cheering for a last-second field goal attempt that may win the game as the clock expires.

All of a sudden a drive through Canada in the fall to see the leaves change has enormous appeal to you.

Which shouldn't be surprising. You've noticed lately that you're always pointing out the view.

Usually to younger people who don't care.

On the road on business, with the dinner hour approaching and all of your appointments finished, you're in your room watching the news, wearing a T-shirt and a pair of shorts, and you decide to put on a coat and tie and go downstairs to the hotel restaurant and eat by yourself.

Like a little ceremony: dressing for dinner. It would be a lot easier to just have room service sent up. That's what you always used to do. But more and more lately, you actually like sitting alone in a restaurant with a good meal and your thoughts. It's not a consolation prize—at 50, you sort of like your own company.

Although there are nights when you think you can hear the theme from *Driving Miss Daisy* playing somewhere in the restaurant.

The sweet concept of stopping to smell the roses, you have noticed at 50, seems to have been irrevocably amended.

It's a laudable idea—the smelling-the-roses part has great appeal. It's the having-to-stop-to-do-it part that seems outdated. Today every implicit instinct is that it can be done more efficiently. Move the cursor down to the "roses" position on the solid-state disk, store the roses in your own file, give yourself the option of being able to call up the roses when you have the time to smell them.

The alleged advances in the world are changing the texture of life, even when you don't want it to happen. You look at a sunset, and it's beautiful, and as the sun sinks you have the impulse that you ought to hit the "rewind" button so you can see it again. That you should point a zapper at the setting sun and move it back a little higher in the sky while in the "search" mode, so that you can freeze it at exactly the spot where you want the sunset to recommence. The idea that certain things in life must be taken slowly and on their own time, that they can happen once and only once—that you can't reverse tonight's sunset—is going away. We have been taught that we can alter anything, and though we know we can't, it feels thus even as the sun drops below the horizon.

That little red convertible?

The one you want to drive around town?

Your desire to drive that little red car has nothing to do with a midlife crisis, or a search for lost youth, or anything remotely similar.

The reason you want to drive that car is that you really like the idea of driving that car.

And you have come to realize that if you resist the urge to drive the car this summer, then you'll probably resist the urge next summer, too, and the summer after that. And by resisting the urge, you will in effect be guaranteeing that you will never drive that red convertible.

It's as simple as that.

So you choose to drive it. Now.

The news of a hot new restaurant opening in town leaves you cold.

You have calmly reached the conclusion that there is really nothing a restaurant can offer that you have not eaten in a restaurant or seen in a restaurant in your fifty years on Earth. You'll be happy to drop by the new place after the lines have disappeared. Give the restaurant a little time to simmer down.

It won't be new by then—but neither are you.

I was staying in a hotel that was serving as host to a sales meeting of a large corporation; on the last night, after the business part was done, an outdoor banquet was held for all who were attending.

The party had a pirate motif; the actors and actresses who were dressed as pirates fired starter's guns to signal that dinner was being served.

And the smell of the smoke from the starter's pistols . . .

It was the smell of Norwoods—the run-down amusement park in the town where I was a boy. Norwoods is long gone now, and I hadn't thought about it in thirty years. But the smoke from the blanks in the pirates' starter's pistols, the smell of the impotent gunpowder, was the smell of the old shooting gallery at Norwoods, and walking past a sales conference of which I was not a part, it carried me back over all those years. At 50, the sights and sounds and fragrances of remembered fun are as vivid as today's six o'clock newscast, and we don't mind it at all, debilitated gunpowder at sunset, we welcome it and try to figure out a way to say that we want more.

Speaking of amusement parks:

Theme-park America seems to operate on the all-you-can-eat principle: Charge the customers too much, and send them home for the day with their entertainment plates still not empty, and they won't complain.

So a family of four can spend $300 for a day at a famous theme park, and walk away grateful. But fun is not quantifiable; the price of fun cannot be calibrated. On summer nights when I was 15 or 16, when there were no theme parks within the realm of possibility, we would go out on the 3-C Highway to a place called Bounceland. Bounceland consisted of a series of shallow pits, each covered with a tautly pulled sheet of hard rubber. These were low-rent trampolines; for fifty cents per half hour, you could bounce atop the holes in the central Ohio earth.

Bounceland advertised on local radio stations, a happy jingle set to a cheery tune: *Bounceland, bounce your troubles away* . . .

Fifty cents. That's what it cost to make us smile. Expectations, and the scale of joy, and what it takes to make a memory . . .

At 50, so many years and so many dollars spent in the pursuit of bliss, and what is it we have been chasing all these years? A means. A method. To bounce our troubles away . . .

Dessert, you realize once again, has become a morality play.

Before you sit down to dinner, you tell yourself that no dessert, regardless of how alluring, has the potential to give you enough pleasure to make up for the extra pound you will have to face in the morning. Dessert is a waste; dessert does nothing for you.

Then, as dinner's main course is ending, you become irrationally angry. At yourself, at the world, at the circumstances. "What, I'm going to look so much better in the morning if I *don't* eat dessert? At this stage in my life I don't deserve this *one simple thing*? I'm going to be so much better off if I *deprive* myself?"

Life seemed more placid when it didn't require the talents and insights of William Faulkner to adequately capture all the emotion and angst of whether you should order a piece of fudge cake.

The great fallacy of money is that all of the things during your life for which you worried you overpaid a little bit—cars, vacations, meals, family weekends away—and all of the things you congratulated yourself for getting what you thought was a great deal on—television sets, living room furniture, tires . . .

None of it matters. All of the money you thought you got finagled out of, all of the money you thought you pocketed in smart deals, means nothing. It's all a wash. All that bargaining and all that effort, and now, at 50, you know it was all wasted energy. You should have concentrated on having a good time. The good times, or their absence, are all that is left. Isn't that something? The money didn't matter.

So what does matter? What are the things that really count?

I was on a trip, feeling a little down about something, and I called my best friend from back when I was a kid. Even though we live in different towns now, we still can talk to each other with the unguardedness of when we were 5 years old.

I called him around 10 P.M. his time. We have always known each others' voices instantly, but this time, after he had picked up the phone and said hello and I had said "Hi," he said, with a question mark in his voice, "Who's this?" I was surprised he would ask. I told him who it was.

"I thought so," he said. "But then I wasn't sure, because you never call this late at night."

That's what counts. A person who knows you so well that he knows what you never do. In a world that doesn't always care.

•   •   •

And:

Another very good friend, one I have known since college, lives in St. Louis. We keep in close touch, sometimes talking on the phone a couple of times a week. But we're seldom in the same city.

One summer night I did find myself in St. Louis on business, and in the middle of the evening, when my work was done, he and I got together and went out for a sandwich. I still had one eye on the work I'd just completed and one eye on the deadline just ahead; he was running late to get home to his family. So we talked and had a good time, laughed and told stories, and he dropped me back at my hotel and as I got out of the car he said something.

"There's got to be a better way than this," he said. "We're about as good friends as either of us has. And we see each other every year and a half, for an hour and a half. And the whole time, we're looking at the clock and going to the phone to check for messages. This is the best we can do?"

If it is, at 50, we—all of us—owe it to ourselves to figure out a way to do it better. To defeat the futility that seems ever inherent in the things that should mean the most.

Perhaps that is so important now because we are entering the senior-year phase of our lives.

It's different from being senior citizens. That's yet to come. But the senior-year phase has to do with you knowing that if certain experiences don't work out this time, you're not going to have the chance to get them back.

When you were 18 and literally a senior—a senior in high school—that meant football games and Homecoming dances and summers with your friends. You knew, that year, that you'd better get it right, because it was about to go away.

Now you're 50, but you still have the feeling. The successes of family vacations and dinners with people you care for matter to you more not because you've become more critical or demanding. You get annoyed if something goes wrong during these times not because you're suddenly churlish or unreasonable.

You're this way because you sense that a lot of this stuff isn't going to come around again. This is it. You need for it to be OK.

I woke up in the middle of the night, couldn't get back to sleep, and turned on the television set. There was an infomercial for a weight-loss product that was called "the AromaTrim Crave Ender."

I had to laugh as I watched the commercial. To help you diet, every time you got hungry you were supposed to take a whiff from a little packet you held in your hand. The smell was supposed to discourage you from eating.

It was a pretty funny thing to watch, the people whiffing away at their AromaTrim Crave Enders. I turned the TV set off with a smile on my face.

Only later did I think: That's what we all may turn out to need, isn't it. A Crave Ender. Not necessarily for a diet. Just to diminish all the craving. All the wanting. Including, perhaps, the wanting that keeps us awake in the middle of the night.

Symphony music sounds pretty good to you suddenly.

And you have a renewed desire to have a home aquarium. The fish, with their colors and their motion, relax you.

At 50 you decide that Labor Day shouldn't be called a holiday.

Not out of any disrespect for the labor pioneers the day is supposed to commemorate; it's fine to have the day off. It's the timing of Labor Day that has become symbolic to you. The timing makes it feel like the most melancholy holiday of all. Summer's over. The warmth is done with, the cold is about to begin.

At 50 your unspoken goal is to keep your life from feeling like Labor Day has arrived—to push the Labor Day feeling as far away from you as you can. To hold off the time when you must face that post–Labor Day feeling: The air is turning chilly, the good times are winding down.

That's no holiday. In the calendar of your time on Earth, there is no place for Labor Day. At least not yet.

Starting early in a person's life, there is a desire to join things—clubs that will confer admission and membership, letting the person know that he or she has qualified, has been accepted.

The need for this kind of outside judgment diminishes considerably by 50. Which is one of the great, serious, and quiet satisfactions of the age: the realization that there is no one who can give you a truer evaluation of your worth than you.

14

Hope Is Right Around the Corner

Hope, at 50, takes many forms.

I once spoke with Jack Kramer, the great tennis player of the 1940s and early 1950s. As celebrated as Kramer was for his championships on the court, his real fame came from the tennis racket named in his honor: the Wilson Jack Kramer Autograph.

For any kid growing up wanting to be a tennis player in the fifties and sixties, owning a Kramer—that's how players referred to them—was a rite of passage. Between 1949, when Wilson introduced the Kramers, and 1981, when they were eliminated from Wilson's line, more than 10 million were sold.

The Kramers were eventually done away with because they were made out of wood. By the eighties, metal and graphite rackets had ascended, and the Kramers were no longer selling well.

But even at the end, they were still an attractive purchase for one person:

"When they closed them all out, I said that I wanted to buy some," Jack Kramer told me. "They said they'd sell them to me for eight dollars a racket, unstrung. They were all in a warehouse down in Tennessee. I bought 300 of them. I'm down to about 175 now. I've given a lot away. Some people say that they just can't play tennis without a wooden Kramer, so when I hear that, I just give them one. The 175 that I have left are stacked in the garage and in the back bedroom."

Why? Hope—the hope of a kind of immortality. Kramer said that he had given Wilson the right to make a contract with his estate after his death, and, if the company wished, to begin producing Jack Kramer Autograph rackets again. "To have people playing with Kramers after I'm gone— what a thrill to think of that."

Hope—it seems only to get stronger.

You can see it in the smallest moments.

On a summer morning you go out for a walk, and clouds and haze block the sun. You pass someone else who is out walking. "The fog's supposed to burn off by noon," the person says.

We all believe it. Even on the last day of a vacation that's been gloomy and gray. Even at 50, when all recent events would argue otherwise. "The fog's supposed to burn off." Among the most optimistic words in the English language.

You don't think there's hope in life? You, at 50, don't believe good things can happen?

A guy who went to my high school owns Victoria's Secret.

•   •   •

People tend to shift their ambition into overdrive at 50 for a specific and understandable reason. It's this:

All during a person's life, he thinks that right around the corner is the good thing he's going to find. That metaphorical corner is a given—your life is an endless succession of streets and corners, and you never know what's coming next, but you really do believe that when you turn one of those corners the ultimate wonderful thing will be waiting for you.

And then your personality begins to change a little bit, because you start to think: If it's not around that corner up there—that next corner, the one you can see—it may not be out there after all.

The succession of corners doesn't seem endless anymore. The corners don't reach all the way to the horizon. The corners ahead of you, for the first time, seem to be running out. They're finite.

And it makes you different, in ways that are good and in ways you sense are perhaps not so good.

Hope can present itself in ways that are quietly heroic.

I interviewed a man in a small Ohio town about some subject or other, and when we were done with the interview he told me that he had to go take his dance lesson.

He was in his 50s; he had lost his wife, and was struggling with the new circumstance of being a widower. His nights had become empty, and he hadn't been sure what to do about it.

So he had enrolled in a ballroom dancing class—if I remember correctly, it was one of the Arthur Murray franchises. The class was up a staircase above a store in his town. It took a certain courage for him to do this—to go to the class and sign up for the dancing lessons, knowing that he would be admitting something about his solitude, and his unsureness of where to go in his life, and his need.

And his hope. He told me he had to get to class. As if saying that was just some throwaway sentence.

"A lifelong friend."

You've been using that phrase for so long that it's a little jarring when you stop to ask yourself: Is it still possible to develop a lifelong friendship now? At 50, if you meet a person and get along well, and keep getting along well from now on in, does that qualify as a lifelong friendship? Or not—has the starting point for friendships that can be considered lifetime already passed?

You hope not.

In a yard, children are playing, and you see one boy with a bright-eyed look, trying to get the attention of the others.

They aren't taking any note of him at all. But his eyes are still bright—he's still young enough to believe that when the other children see that he is motioning to them, they will welcome him and include him and bring him into their game.

The eyes are so bright they just about glisten. They're happy, trusting eyes. That trust—that trust and that hope— has not been stepped on yet. You, at 50, look at him, and you think about how fine a world it would be if no one's early hope was ever stepped on, if the eyes were allowed to remain eternally so bright and unclouded.

Does hope really spring eternal?

Something does. How else would you explain your pathetic eagerness to find out what the soup of the day is?

•   •   •

There was a time, long ago, when you had never kissed anyone.

It seemed impossible. It seemed like climbing Pikes Peak. You could barely imagine what that day would be like—how you would ever be able to pull it off. The anticipation, the hope, the newness, the wanting it to happen . . .

At 50, it seems like forever ago. But if you can ever get that feeling back—not about kissing someone (well, not *necessarily* about kissing someone), but about *something*, about something in your life over which you can work up the will-I-ever-kiss-someone longing . . .

If you can bring that kind of hope back into your life over something, you will have won.

Hope can be mundane. That doesn't mean it isn't hope.

You walk through the aisles of a grocery store. The various breads are displayed in their wrappers: white, rye, raisin, cinnamon, pumpernickel, on and on.

At 50, you look at each loaf of bread as if it has as much potential to provide enjoyment as a birthday party.

That onion bread . . . is that new this week?

Occasionally you stop and think about whether there will ever be any new musical hits for us.

At 50, people talk about "our music," and what they're almost always referring to is oldies. Beatles, Beach Boys, Rolling Stones, all the rest . . . "our music," in the vernacular, happened many years ago.

You'd think it wouldn't have to be that way. You'd think there will come a time—at 50 and after—when we will rush out and buy a new record album because the songs speak to us, move us, address our yearnings and our fears the same way our music did when we were first loving music. That someone—you wish Brian Wilson would somehow be able to do it once again—will write the music that will put our feelings, the way they are today, into three-minute guitar-and-vocal novels.

Because we need the things the music can give us now every bit as much as we needed it then. Maybe more.

I have some friends, a couple who—concerned about the growing rate of crime in their community—bought a home security system for the first time.

When the wiring of their house was completed, the alarm company instructed them to enter a code number into the keypad by their front door—a number they can routinely tap in to activate or turn off the alarms.

The code they put in was the birthday of their youngest daughter—the numerical month, day, and year of her birth.

Their daughter's birthday coded into the security alarm. Her parents' fears and hopes mixed all together, a complicated sign of where they are in their lives.

The people who, in middle age, take college and adult education classes:

What exactly is it they are seeking?

Lifelong learning, of course. Yet the question is, what do they hope to do with what they learn? Most of the courses—at least the ones that aren't trade-school stuff, not training for their careers—tend to be fairly esoteric, with little evident real-world value.

Which may be the answer. Adult education classes are a reverse spin on the you-can't-take-it-with-you thought. When it comes to money, "you can't take it with you" means that you'd better spend it now, have all the good times you can. With learning, it's your ignorance—too harsh a word; it's your lack of knowledge—that you can't, and don't want to, take with you. So you fill that vacuum up. You give yourself all the knowledge you have missed out on, not because there's any reason for you to know these things, but because not having a reason to know them is the best reason of all.

Plus, you're always looking to get back that New Student Week feeling. Even at 50.

You would probably have guessed, earlier in your life, that by 50 or thereabouts the time would come for sitting back, counting up, serenely compiling the ledger of what you have accomplished.

That prediction would have made sense. All predictions do—until you get to the place you're making the predictions about. When you get to that place—when you get to 50—you find you have absolutely no desire to add up your successes and take a look at the tally. You shake off the very thought.

Because to do that would be like letting the clock run out while you're still on the field. Wait a minute—this game's not over yet. This game can still be won—how many time-outs have we got left? You're not going to the locker room just yet—not even thinking about it. As soon as someone starts talking to you about the final score, you discover that you're not anywhere near as tired as you'd thought you were. Tired? You can still put this game into overtime.

Which may have something to do with why that Army commercial—"Be All That You Can Be"—strikes you much differently than it did when the message was first broadcast.

It's intended for the 19-year-old mind. "Be All That You Can Be" is a brilliant slogan to get 19-year-olds revved up for life. Everything's stretching out ahead, there for the taking and the molding.

At 50 the same words sound like an indictment, or at least a taunting goad. "Be All That You Can Be" translates to: Is that it? Is that all you've been able to accomplish? Are you satisfied with this?

It can still work—the slogan can still get you moving. But instead of the unseen drill sergeant at the starting line, telling the 19-year-olds to go out and run the race as well as they can, now that invisible sergeant is standing just up the stretch from the finish line, staring at his stopwatch and shaking his head in disapproval. Meaning for you to see him do it—meaning for you to find the wind for a renewed sprint, to understand that whatever it is you're going to be, this last dash is where you'll find the answer.

Sometimes hope is something you're best advised to apply not to a distant shore in your undefined future, but—with a smile—to right this second.

The smile is because there are times when, right this second, you feel objectively lousy. Your back aches, your allergies are acting up, you can't make out the names and numbers in the telephone book. What is there in *that* that could possibly make you feel OK?

What there is is this: that recurrent realization of yours that as bad as you feel right now, this may be as good as you're ever going to feel. Even if your back doesn't deteriorate even more, your allergies don't get even more annoying, your eyesight doesn't get even more fuzzy, the chances aren't good that they're going to get all that better, either. The best you can count on is a draw.

Truthfully—what do you think the odds are that, however you're feeling this morning, you're going to feel *much, much* better when you're 70 or 72?

So however you're feeling today, take a breath and enjoy it. These may be the good old days sooner than you think.

(Although, in the back of your mind, you're still count-ing on the day, somewhere up the road, when all the feel-ings you have are the feelings you had as a kid on a sunny summer morning. That's the definition of hope at 50—your belief, in the face of everything, that the summer morning, and all it represented, is coming. Any day now.)

A friend showed me a picture of his daughter.

She was, I believe, 13. In the picture she is crossing a city street. The other people with her in the photo—the other people who are crossing the downtown street—do not real-ize that her picture is being taken by her dad on the other side.

Her arms are pumping in an exaggerated manner; the closed-lipped smile on her face and the look in her eyes speak of a secret joke between her and her father. If you didn't know the girl, this would be just another street scene. For this family, though, it means something. Their daugh-ter—a person among people on that particular street. No longer a little girl—a person downtown.

The photograph, I would guess, will end up under glass on top of a dresser in her father's and mother's bedroom. Where do the children go? Leaving home soon, entering the world, the world of all those people on all those streets. The people who, long ago and not so long ago, stepped alone onto those downtown streets for the first time, too.

You can't make time stop. As hard as you want to, you can't do it. Where do the children go? On the street in the picture his daughter is no longer a child.

"I've got a new doctor. I told him what pills I was taking, and he said, 'Are you *crazy*?' "

I heard the woman—around 50—saying this with funny intent. She was, on the surface, making fun of both the doctor and the situation. The doctor hears her pill menu and jokes that she's crazy for taking all that stuff together.

But behind the words is something else—hope. Hope in a new doctor. A new doctor who is probably younger than she is. A person doesn't go to a doctor because she is feeling good—there may be a smile in her voice as she tells the story now, but no one, at 50, makes an appointment with the doctor for the fun of it.

She's wanting something. Most likely what she wants is for her new doctor to tell her what she is doing wrong, and to tell her that if she will only do the things he says are right, she'll be OK. Her new young doctor, she hopes, will change the things in her life that are causing her worry; that's why she has sought him out.

Now, though—the first appointment over—she says the words lightly, as if she is setting up a punch line:

"I've got a new doctor. I told him what pills I was taking . . ."

You hear a couple of 50-year-old guys saying that they're going fishing tomorrow, and finally, after all these years, you know what fishing is.

The perfect allegory for life: trying to reel in something of worth, something unseen. Chasing down a rumor of goodness out there, the fishermen cast their lines and finger their reels. At this very moment the fish are as good as they're ever going to be, because the men can't see them. Right now the fish, their size, their heft, exist only in the men's imaginations.

All of us, fishing every day. And we choose to call it something else.

Annals of Pathos:

Your shirts come back from the laundry in those little

shirt bags that are paper in the back and see-through semi-plastic on the front. On that semi-plastic front is a drawing of a butler, with the words: "Your shirt, sir."

And you think: Now there's someone who knows how to treat the customer with respect. There's someone I like doing business with.

You're having these thoughts about a picture on a shirt bag.

You still, despite everything, believe in the last dance.

There was a time when it carried such weight. Last dance—when you were young, and the party was about to end, who you danced the last dance with—or whether you danced it at all—was the measuring rod of the evening. No matter what else had happened during the night, the last dance had the potential to send you home happy or empty.

You don't dance anymore. The idea of the last dance signifies something far different to you now than it did then. But the party is starting to show signs of winding down. At 50, you've got your eye on the last dance. You want to make it mean something.

I saw a man out walking on the beach, wearing a baseball cap that said "55 and Up," the left side of the "U" in the word "Up" an arrow pointing toward the sky.

I saw another man wearing a sweatshirt that said, on the front, "It Took Me 70 Years to Look This Good."

You know the clothing is intended as a joke, at least a mild one, but you also know that beneath the joke there is something else. Some people—you among them—would never wear the cap or the shirt. But even the men and women who don't wear the slogans are on some level thinking the thoughts.

"55 and Up." "It Took Me 70 Years to Look This Good."

It's only something to be smirked at by kids who aren't yet aware that they, too, are on their way to this beach. They'll get here sooner than they know.

When I was a child I had an aunt named Rosina. On every birthday—sixth, seventh, eighth, ninth—she would give me a card. Inside the card she would have written:

"Eight years old! Eight is the best year of all."

And I believed it. For a number of years there, I believed she must be telling the truth. The best year of all? If Aunt Rosina said so, it must be correct.

She left this Earth some time ago. And now when a birthday rolls around I sometimes think of her, and I also think:

She wouldn't be telling me this now. When you have your birthday in middle age, you know when you wake up that birthday morning that it's probably not going to be the start of the best year of all. Those birthdays—the best-year birthdays—are gone.

Not that you don't hold out the hope that this year will be the best one. You could, indeed, have your best year of all starting today. But from now on in, if you do, it will be unexpected, an anomaly. You may be hopeful—everyone you know may be hopeful, on all of the birthdays to come. But no one ever says in advance that 57 is the best year in a man's or a woman's life.

At 50, the sound of a one-way ticket is suddenly enticing.

You have spent your entire adult life assuming that your tickets will be round-trip. That they will always have the built-in potential to bring you home.

But at 50, the concept of a one-way trip—a trip to a place you've never been, a place where you might fantasize about staying and starting over—has an allure. For the first time, the phrase "one-way ticket out of here" does not feel like a threat.

It sounds like a promise.

One piece of our lives showing that, deep down, we were always hoping:

This generation—the generation turning 50 now—used to be depicted in those newsreels of elementary school children crouching under their desks during atomic bomb drills. The deep voice of the newsreel narrator said that we were a generation of children growing up in fear—that because the adult leaders of the world could not solve their problems, we had to go to school scared, never knowing when the Civil Defense air-raid siren might go off.

The secret is that we never believed it. The secret is that it wasn't all that scary. When it was time for an A-bomb drill, we sort of liked it. It got us out of doing classwork for fifteen minutes or so.

We knew the Russians weren't coming. But we crawled under those desks like veterans of the Battle of Britain. You can still see us in those old pictures. Trying to look appropriately frightened.

15

"Those Guys Must Be Having So Much Fun"

Of all the questions for which you are supposed to have the answers, it sometimes seems that the most complicated is the one that should be the simplest: the question of who you are. Who you really are.

It's a question that can raise its head at unexpected times. I was back in my hometown, helping out with a fund-raiser for the public school system. One of the things I was supposed to do was give brief talks to all the different grades of schoolchildren. They assembled in the elementary school auditorium at times throughout the day.

So I was standing on the stage toward which I had looked during all my own years in the school—the stage where the school plays were held, the stage where the principal had welcomed us back early each September, the stage above which a projection screen could be pulled down for noon movies.

The first groups of students were brought in—kinder-garteners through third graders—and I looked out at them, so early in their lives, so unformed and eager, with almost everything they encountered being new to them. I told some stories and gave a little speech, and then I asked if there were any questions.

A child stood up and said, "Is there anything you still wish you could do?"

And without even being aware I was saying the words, I said: "Yes. I wish I could be you."

At least for that moment, I meant it. I didn't want to be the person on the stage, attempting to pass knowledge down. I wanted to be in the seats, with all of life ahead of me.

There is a story that Paul Simon and Art Garfunkel tell.

In the story, as they remember it, they have made their first record. They have grown up listening to other singers on the radio, thinking of the grand and exciting lives those singers are leading. Now they have done it themselves—they have gotten a recording contract, and their first song has been pressed.

So one night they are sitting outside in the town where they live—still very young men—and the radio is playing, and their record comes on. Their song is on the air, in this town, on this night.

And one of them looks at the other and says:

"Those guys must be having so much fun."

It's an emotion that all of us feel, in varying degrees, throughout our adult lives. Who is the person the world thinks you are? And is that the same person who is inside you? Which one are you? The one they see, or the one you feel? Every person, at 50, deals with that every time he or she walks out the door and into the world.

Those guys must be having so much fun. We believe it about others, even while knowing the chanciness of assuming it about ourselves.

You go through your closets and drawers, and if you're a 50-year-old man you find yourself grinning at some of the old jackets, ties, shirts and pants that are in there; if you're a 50-year-old woman you find yourself smiling at some of the dresses, skirts, blouses and slacks.

It's not that there's anything inherently funny about the clothes you find in your closet; it's not even that the clothes went out of style.

It's that, on the day you bought them, you thought they would make you look better. That had to be the reason you chose them and you purchased them—to improve your look. The *clothes* aren't funny. You are.

You, on this lifelong quest to make yourself look good.

By the swimming area of a resort hotel, I saw a man talking to his wife.

"Jacob and Rosalie are in the pool?" he said.

She nodded yes and pointed to the children.

The man had that businessman-on-vacation look. And I thought: He may not know it, but of all the sentences he will speak this week—all the checking into the office through cellular phones, all the instructions given to subordinates over long-distance—those words he has just spoken are the most important words.

The inflection, the question mark ending a sentence that's not technically a question—"Jacob and Rosalie are in the pool?"—the downplayed concern inherent in the words, the assumption in those words and at the same time the vigilance . . .

Those are the words that matter. A father speaking of his

children, children who have names like grandparents. A small and almost silent moment, lost in the warm breeze.

They're 50 and they're talking over dinner in a restaurant. Two couples.

One of the men says:

"This guy's a top guy. We heard that he was only doing hips."

The knowing nods from the others at the table, the overlapping words of approval. These are people who, not so very long ago, would have been having the same animated, interested discussion about the hidden meanings in the lyrics on a new Bob Dylan album.

A woman at the table says:

"Well, I wouldn't want anybody doing my knee who's been doing only hips."

Who we all are; who we all were. The waitress comes around to ask if anyone would like dessert. They wave her off like four overzealous umpires signaling a runner is safe at home.

You're back in your hometown, and you run into an old man. He was your family's neighbor when you were growing up.

You look at him and you remember how important it was, when you were 10 or 11, to make the neighbors think highly of you, to impress them with your worth, your brightness, your athletic aptitude. Maybe even more important than impressing your own family. Because when you're that young—although you're not aware of it at the time—trying to make the neighborhood adults think well of you is your first sense of wanting to make a good impression on the outside world. And the only outside world available to you is the immediate world outside the walls of your parents' house.

You're 50 years old now. You're thinking all these things as you see your parents' old neighbor again. You have the impulse to try to put your thoughts into words.

He speaks first.

"Well, it's been a long time," he says.

What you say is:

"Yes, it has been a long time."

Which will have to do.

And:

On those trips back to your hometown, when you see the high school coaches you knew as a kid, and the civic figures—the mayor from your childhood—you automatically call them "Mr.," and they laughingly tell you that's not necessary. They tell you that it's OK to call them by their first names now; they say that you don't have to call them "Mr." anymore.

Well, yes, you do.

If not for them, then for you. Maybe they don't feel the need for you to call them "Mr." But you feel the need. At 50, you still want someone in your life to be "Mr." to you. They're the ones. Now and always.

Among the everyday concepts you have seen go away since you were a kid is—both in reality and in symbol—the attic.

The attics of houses were places where people actually went—crawling through a hole in a bedroom closet or walking up a flight of stairs hidden behind its own door. The attics were storage places for bits of life the family did not have room for downstairs, bits of life the family no longer required daily use of, but did not want to part with. Attics were repositories of a family's history—history that was often destined never to be seen again, packed away in boxes or jammed into dusty corners. But there, nevertheless.

The attic, and all that it entails, is mostly gone from the national landscape. There don't seem to be as many literal attics.

Yet much of your life, you realize, is in an attic of your own devising—an attic inside of you. The place where the things with which you will not part are stored and waiting, just in case.

All these years after we first learned how to do it, we're all still very proficient at the we-just-happened-to-be-walking-by pose.

It serves the same purpose it always has: to mask everything. Desire, and wanting, and feeling the wish to be included. We make sure we are present, there to be noticed; we make plans and get ready and show up on time, and then we stand there, as if we just happened to be passing through. Just—by some odd circumstance—happened to be in this place at this moment.

It's as if we fear that to say how badly we want something tells the world who we are in ways we don't care to admit. This way makes it easier for us. Even at 50. Transparent as it is, we still rely on it. We just happened to be in the neighborhood. But as long as we're here, there's something we'd like.

When you're 6, sometimes you sit outside on a summer day and think about why a stick is called a stick.

It's the kind of thought adults don't have. A stick? A stick is called a stick because . . . well, because a stick is a stick. But when you're 6, this seems like a perfectly logical question to ask yourself. A twig falls off a tree next to your house, and you hold it in your hands and ask yourself: Of all the words that could have been invented to describe this thing, why did "stick" become the one? Who named it stick?

Soon after you turn 7 such thoughts are put away. All through your teenage years, and into college, out into the working world, the beginnings of your career and the various ups and downs, there are so many more important things to occupy your mind. Relationships and family responsibilities and job decisions and travel plans and financial gains and reversals. All of them so consuming of your attention, all of them—at least briefly—so significant.

At 50, you see a stick on the ground and you pick it up. Now, why—you ask yourself—is this thing called a stick? Who decided to name it that? Why that particular word?

The world revolves on its axis. You ponder this thing that is called a stick.

The "those were great days" way of seeing things is something you try your hardest to avoid.

It's an easy hole to trip into, especially at 50. The high points of your life up until now—personal triumphs, business victories, moments that felt the most fulfilling—have been building up since you were a young person. The temptation is always there to sit back and think of those great days—to recall them fondly, and pat yourself on the back for having lived them.

But some voice inside tells you that as soon as you do that—as soon as you become one of the "those were great days" people—you are giving yourself an excuse for not making today, and tomorrow, great days. That every day spent reminiscing about something in the past that has gone well is a day when you are neglecting to make sure something new goes well.

Occasionally you ask yourself what would be so wrong

with savoring the "those were great days" days; what would the difference be if you allowed yourself that kind of reflective satisfaction? After all, many people do.

But you fight it. There will be time for that later.

Assuming you will allow yourself to allow it even then.

In a world that seems to honor only the yammering and the boisterous, where the loud voices are never lowered and the soft voices are never heard, you ask yourself whether even Dick Vitale and Charles Barkley ever secretly wish that they were Gary Cooper.

Because you realize that Gary Cooper was the American ideal precisely because he didn't have to say much. Not only did Cooper not feel the need to raise his voice—in his most effective moments he didn't say anything at all.

Of course, he was up there on that screen, which helped. He didn't have to try to attract anyone's attention, because he knew that all of America was out there in the theater seats, having chosen to stare at his illuminated image on the screen.

And today, you think, even the screens aren't nearly as big as they were when they contained Gary Cooper, framed and centered and quiet.

If you threw away everything—your clothes, your book full of addresses and telephone numbers, your personal papers, your files, everything—and just started over, how would you do?

What would it be like, to have that clean slate? Does the thought of it make you feel scared? Does the thought of it sound fun? Terrible? Great?

What do you think your prospects would be, if you could do that tomorrow morning? How would you do?

Who would you be?

• • •

On a Friday night, in a town not your own, you are driving along a street and you look over and see that the street borders a high school football stadium.

In a wink of an instant you take it all in: the lights from the towers, and the high murmur of the constant sound, and the hazy glow in the air. It's like being in a time machine—this is what autumn Friday nights felt like when Friday nights were first special to you, this is a taste of the sensory feast you once looked forward to all week. In your car you hear the sound rise—someone must have just made a long run or caught a pass—and that glow in the night air comes right through the front-seat window, beckoning to you. All you have to do is pull over and buy a ticket and walk right in.

You're 50. You don't stop. You drive on down the street.

"Is this the entrance to the restaurant?"

I was standing on the back terrace of a hotel on a warm spring night. The man asking the question had walked up with a friend—both men appeared to be in their 70s. Old friends wanting to have dinner.

It wasn't a restaurant they were peering into—it was a function room where a corporate event was going on. I explained what the gathering was.

"So it's a big party?" the second man said.

"No," I said, "it's a business meeting," worrying that my words sounded patronizing even as they left my mouth. *It's a business meeting*—as in, this is business, you wouldn't understand. To men who probably had spent forty years or more in the business world. I felt like apologizing, but they seemed not to notice.

"Well, we'll just find a place to eat, then," the first man said.

Old friends, and as I looked at them walk away I thought about my own best friend from my college years, and of all the nights during school when we used to head out, two guys looking for a place to have dinner. As I saw the two men at this hotel move gingerly across the terrace, it occurred to me that my old best friend and I are now much closer in age to those two men than we are to the young men we used to be in school.

The aisles in front of the self-improvement shelves in America's bookstores are almost always occupied. Even on slow days in the stores, when the fiction and biography sections are devoid of customers, there are people leafing through the self-help books.

Apparently it never goes away—this impulse that begins so early, this impulse to do better. Young people are thinking about it years before they'd ever buy a book to advise them on how to improve—and people who would never buy one of those books are thinking about it, too.

Which may or may not be a hopeful sign. But it does, at 50, raise the question:

When does the day come when you feel that you're as good as you're ever going to get?

Or does that day never quite roll around?

"I'm going to go over to Titusville tomorrow morning to watch the shuttle go up."

He was talking about the space shuttle. The man who was speaking to me—a cabdriver in Florida—said that he and his wife were going to leave their own town just after midnight, drive across the state to Titusville, where, they had been told, they could get a clear sightline of the shuttle blasting off from Cape Canaveral.

He was going to do it, and I never had. It's the Africa and

Paris dilemma of life; from the time you are a child you realize that Africa is there, and Paris is there, and you just sort of assume you'll get there one day to see them. And at 50, if you've never done it, you begin to realize for the first time that you probably never will. That Africa and Paris were in the geography books and on the maps of the world before you were born, and that they'll be there after you're gone, and that if you don't get yourself there, no one but you will ever know. Africa won't care. Paris won't care. It's not as if they can invite you to come, although you may have always half-believed that's how it worked. There are no invitations. You work up the initiative to go, or the going never happens. Your absence will not be noted.

Same with the blastoffs from Cape Canaveral. The exploration of space has been the great experiment of our century—maybe the greatest single accomplishment. And now that it's winding down—no more of those moon shots—if you've never gone to see it happen, you most likely never will.

I never have. Why?

Probably I was waiting for the nonexistent invitation. "We're going to pack sandwiches," the cabdriver told me, looking beyond his windshield. In a way many of us fail to do.

What we don't fail to do, however—although failing to do it might be a good idea—is to look in the mirror first thing every morning.

That initial sight is like a pitcher of ice water tossed in the face of one's who-I-really-am quandary. Because when you close your eyes and think of yourself, the vision you conjure up is some relatively pleasant if slightly older version of the thirty-five-years-ago you getting ready to go out to join your best friends. You know the years have gone by, but that's still the person you think you are.

And then, at 7 A.M. or thereabouts—the worst time for looking at yourself—you glance into the mirror, and even the face of Bela Lugosi would be preferable to what you see.

Because the person who greets you instead of Bela—the person who is you—would be, if you were to see the person in a photograph and not in your own mirror, one of millions upon millions of tired, nondescript 50-year-olds in some generational group photo, those people whom younger people look right through, people invisible in their weariness and their wear and tear.

What a thing to wake up to every day. That person in the mirror—how exactly did the person get there?

Certainly not by any choice of yours.

In terms of the celebrated people who have meant something to you—the faraway icons of your lifetime—no new icons can be bigger than the old ones. That's the nature of fame. The first stars to bedazzle you will never be outshone by the stars who are even now entrancing younger generations.

But although those old icons can't be replaced, they can be amplified—the ones you already revere can, against all odds, grow larger still. When I was a boy, my best friend and I would sit through two or three showings of *20,000 Leagues Under the Sea* every weekend during the time it was playing in our local theater. The reason was Kirk Douglas, portraying the heroic seaman Ned Land. Wearing that broadly striped T-shirt, gripping that harpoon, and—most of all—singing "Whale of a Tale" . . . Kirk Douglas was everything a boy could hope to find in an adult movie idol.

Several years ago, *20,000 Leagues Under the Sea* was shown

on network television. I called my old best friend long-distance to tell him it was going to be on (he already knew); he watched in his town and I watched in mine, and when it was over we called each other again. Stunned. Angry. Dismayed.

For—apparently in the interest of fitting the time slot—the network had trimmed Kirk Douglas' rendition of "Whale of a Tale" from the movie.

That indelible scene—Kirk Douglas serenading the other sailors with that unforgettable song—was gone. Out of the TV version of the movie completely.

I wondered whether Kirk Douglas knew. Or if he cared. I had some acquaintances in California who I figured might be in a position to have Kirk Douglas' office phone number. I called them; they did, indeed, have it.

I placed a call to his office and told the secretary why I was calling. Amazingly, Kirk Douglas came onto the line within seconds.

I introduced myself, and asked him whether he'd watched the network's presentation of the movie the night before. He said he hadn't; he'd been out.

I told him what had happened. That "Whale of a Tale" was gone.

There was a silence. Then Kirk Douglas said:

"*What?*"

He couldn't believe it either. And then—this is where the icons-can-get-even-bigger part comes in—he did something that left me numb.

He sang "Whale of a Tale" for me.

Yep. Right there on the phone. Kirk Douglas:

"Got a whale of a tale to tell you lads, a whale of a tale or two . . ."

The whole song. Just for the asking.

You think, at 50, you're finished believing that dreams can come true?

A whale of a tale, and it's all true.

When you think of what your ideal world would look like, you realize that it's painted in colors you haven't thought of in years.

Candy-apple red. Metal-flake blue.

Model-car-paint colors.

For some reason they're popping into your mind again. It's not that you really want your surroundings to be those colors.

At least not yet.

You see the little planes flying over stadiums and beaches, trailing advertising banners behind them. Those planes at one time appeared rather dashing and exotic to you, like something from a movie. Now you know it's not Eddie Rickenbacker up there working the stick and rudder—it's probably some kid who does lawnmower repairs on the days he's not flying.

But once in a while, as you see those planes buzz by, they seem to be the parable for our lives—for all of us, in one way or another. The pilot up there, trailing his advertisement behind him, hoping someone will see it. Not knowing if anyone's looking. But putting out the word, day after day.

Sometimes life is most clearly defined not by what you have achieved, but by what you haven't.

Tim McCarver, the great baseball player, was honored several years ago by his old high school. He'd been an all-around athlete in school, and because he had been applauded so often for his baseball skills, the high school officials thought they'd do something different. They would retire his football number.

The school didn't have a record of what number Mc-Carver had worn on his football jersey. So they wrote to ask him—what number had he worn, so they could retire it?

McCarver didn't remember.

Now . . . most high school athletes never forget what numbers they wore on their uniforms. Well into old age, they tend to bore friends and relatives with tales of their sports achievements. But for someone like McCarver—whose athletic triumphs are only starting, not ending, when he's in school—the uniform number evidently becomes insignificant. He'd gone on to do so much in big-league baseball that his high school football number apparently didn't mean much to him.

But if he'd been cut from his high school team—if he'd been told he wasn't good enough—you can bet that he would recall every detail. The vacuums in a person's life—or so you come to understand at 50—can carry more weight than the parts of life packed full of victories and successes.

Near the water one day, you see a father and his son on the rocks by the shoreline.

The boy is no more than 3. His father is close behind him, but he is letting the child walk on the rocks and find his own way. The boy, walking cautiously and unevenly but obviously proud to be doing this, reaches down to steady himself. As his hand touches the rock, he turns to his father and says: "Cold."

The rock may be cold against his hand, but the child doesn't fall down, and he keeps walking, and it's a fine moment. The father is still just one step behind, there as a safety net. He's given this to his boy—this day out on the rocks, a day to find out what it feels like to be on his own.

You watch the father and the son, and you realize what is starting for the boy. Because you're him—you're that kid, a long, long way from home at 50, out on the rocks by yourself.

Even now, when trying to figure out who we really are, the unexpressed thought is often: "Well, 50's weird, but it's not as weird as we'd thought."

The same way that we have always believed that the mythical good thing may be right around the next corner, we seem also to believe that the truly weird thing—the weirdest thing of all, the thing so weird that it has the potential to make us give up—is around the corner, too.

And we're not at that corner yet.

"Now 60—*that'll* be weird. Sixty will be the weirdest."

We tell ourselves.

For now.

16

Ike's Roads and Bogey's Nights: Going and Staying Put

There used to be a phrase that carried a lot of emotional weight:

"He's really going places!"

It was a vital part of the national ethos, something to be strived for and sought after: the idea that, either literally or symbolically, you were going places. On the move.

At 50, this suddenly seems vastly overrated. Going places is not necessarily something to lust for. Staying put begins to sound not only preferable, but downright lovely.

Part of this has to do with the fact that the world has changed drastically from the days when only the truly lucky were able to save up enough money and arrange the free time to travel widely. Whatever the reason for this shift—cheap airline fares, leisure as a birthright for all—that annoying co-worker munching doughnuts next to you at the

Formica counter of the coffee shop next door to your office building may very well be going to Belgium over Memorial Day weekend. No need for you to go there—you'd only see him.

You can now purchase caps and T-shirts saying that you were anywhere—Vail, the Matterhorn, the University of Notre Dame—without leaving your own town. Souvenirs, which you somehow remember being sold only at the locations whose names they bore, now are as close as your local Sportmart. The world is not a destination, it's an officially licensed property.

Better to just stay home, you often think.

Although home, too, has been altered in definition.

This is mostly the doing of the generation now turning 50. In most towns, life was always defined by that "Oh, that's the Mosers' old house," "Oh, that's the Kaynes' old house" rule of geography—i.e., life was thought of in terms of who used to live in every house on every block. It was a warming way of looking at things—steadiness and continuity were assumed because when you looked at each house, you knew its history. You remembered walking across the front lawn to see someone when you were 6, and when you were 16, and when you were 26. The houses, and the names of the people who lived in them, gave a solid center to your town, and thus to your world—your life.

In recent years, though, we have become people who move around so much, in pursuit of better jobs or simply newer neighborhoods, that the "that's the Feibels' old house" mantra may be going away. As people move every five years or so—or at least enough of them move that they vary the cadence of the town, throw awry its inner clock— the emotional weight of who used to live in each house becomes so light as to approach irrelevance. And as that emotional weight dwindles, so, as we turn 50, does a once taken-for-granted way to connect not only with who we were, but with who we are.

Humphrey Bogart had bored and lonely evenings.

It's something to keep in mind as, at 50, you fight the wandering instincts that used to drive you crazy—the instincts that used to tell you that if you didn't go out and do something, you were missing out.

Ever since you were a kid, you assumed that somewhere out there a party was going on, where everyone was having a great time and laughing and staying up until sunrise. If you weren't at the party, you felt that you were depriving yourself.

Gradually, though, it dawns on you that there had to be nights when even Bogey just came home and read a book and turned in early—and that nights like those are not necessarily without value. You think of Bogey settling in around 9 P.M., quite happy for some solitude and some quiet, and it not only seems acceptable—it seems cool.

The first time I ever was in Beverly Hills I went out for a walk late at night. On a residential street a car stopped for a light. I looked behind the wheel of the car. Driving it was a sleepy-looking Walter Matthau.

Once I was in a hotel bar in Miami, and the guy sitting by himself two stools down was Merlin Olsen. This was when he was doing weekly NFL football broadcasts for NBC—the next day there was going to be a Dolphins game, and here he was, the night before.

On a trip to New York I was waiting in line to check out of my hotel, and the person waiting in front of me was Cary Grant.

What these three little scenes have in common is that

each time I was startled—floored, in the case of Cary Grant. It just seemed like these guys shouldn't have been in these places, doing regular things by themselves and being regular people, with no lights or cameras or announcements of their presence.

But everyone has to be somewhere. Even Cary Grant. It's something to keep in mind the next time you assume that right this moment the really glamorous people are doing something much more exhilarating than you are. (Paul Simon and Art Garfunkel talking: "Those guys must be having so much fun.")

Everyone has to be somewhere. Home is an acceptable somewhere.

For you.

For Bogey.

Not that being at home is always a choice that's available to you. At 50, you can't come close to counting the number of business trips you have gone off on since the days you first started working.

Those first business trips—a plane ticket provided by the company, all your meals paid for, a room in a good hotel— felt better than a promotion. Travel, back then, had the same resonance as a pay raise: The company considered you a special person, and this was one of the ways they showed it—putting you on the road, representing the firm.

Dan Jenkins, the sportswriter-turned-novelist, says that when he was a young newspaper reporter in Fort Worth, Texas, and his sports editor would send him around the state for stories, his lead paragraphs would become more grandiloquent with every mile away from town. Some of the assignments were just day trips, but it didn't matter—they warranted a dateline, and datelined stories by a young traveling sportswriter read differently than stories written when he was back at home. He remembers what he was tempted to make them sound like:

"BEAUMONT—He was an old man who pitched alone in a ballpark only 28 miles from the sea."

"WACO—Call me Ishmael, but only if you can't reach me at the Southwest Conference Track and Field meet."

"SAN ANTONIO—They marched through the old city like a river of steel. You never saw so many golfers in town for the State Junior."

Jenkins says that "it was in my journalistic youth that datelines seemed more important than food, drink, women, cars." That's what business trips first felt like for all of us—like gifts, like votes of corporate confidence.

Now, at 50, business travel is something you want much less of. It has more of the feel of a jail sentence than of anything liberating. When you learn these days that you're supposed to travel for the company, as often as not you flash back to the protest signs you vaguely remember seeing in newspaper photos during the Eisenhower administration, when John Foster Dulles or some other cabinet official was taking off for a foreign journey:

"Is This Trip Necessary?"

At least Dan Jenkins, in his young sportswriting days, presumably knew the names of all the players on all the teams he followed down the Texas highways.

That was another part of what used to be America's sense of place—you had your favorite football and baseball teams, and you knew the names of everyone on them. That's how the team became your favorite—you kept up with the team, season after season, and before long it was as if you knew the players, even though you had never met them.

Today America's disconnectedness is epitomized by its professional sports teams. If you had to name every big-league baseball team without looking at the standings in the morning paper, you probably couldn't—but that's simply because there are so many of them now, due to expansion. When there were eight teams in the National League and eight teams in the American League, you could name them all without having to take a second breath.

And the fact that the ballplayers on today's teams move around constantly, going from team to team like so many steel balls in a pinball machine, is a second, parallel trouble. Free agency may have been a fine development for the players themselves, and for the concept of economic self-determination—but when the athletes whom the citizens of a town care about leave every time they can get a better monetary offer elsewhere, it affects the people who watch them in ways that often are not expressed aloud.

The meaning of a hometown team is diluted when the players are merely highly paid itinerant entertainers. Hometown teams—even in hometowns as large as New York and Chicago—meant what they did because the fans knew that they could come to the ballpark day after day, season after season, year after year, and the players they loved would be there. It was close to a feeling of family, something that grew slowly over time. A season would end, the months would go by, the new season would start—and the fans would be back, a little older, and there, down on the field, would be the players, the familiar faces, those faces also a little older . . . but present and accounted for.

When that changed—when the presumption became that once a season was over, that particular squad was probably over forever, too—the meaning of sports also changed. For if few of us stay in one place anymore in our real lives, and we can't count on the players on our favorite teams to stay in one place, either . . .

Well, the constancy ends. We've known for a while that

we don't have as much of it in our individual lives as we might want. We don't have it in sports, either. The players we are supposed to be loyal to pack up at season's end, en route to some other team's clubhouse, where a different uniform is waiting. Is this trip necessary?

You may, at 50, be a person who is always early to the airport for your flight—sitting in the boarding area waiting as the gate agent unlocks the drawer and announces that he's ready to check the tickets.

You may, at 50, be a person who is always late to the airport for your flight—rushing through the terminal, looking at your watch to see if you're going to make it, arriving at the gate just as the door to the plane is about to close.

If you're one of the early arrivers, you can be just about certain that, for the remainder of your life, you will never be late for a flight. If you're one of the late arrivers, you can be just about certain that, for the remainder of your life, you will never get there with plenty of time to spare. That's a given now. These little things—little things like your airport arrival habits; thousands of little things that, in combination, define you—are set now. They are you.

For now and always. If there was ever a time when these things were going to change, that time seems to be gone. These aren't quirks. They are who you are. Hope you like them.

The rudest innovation of our lifetimes is call waiting.

To satisfy the purpose of making your life allegedly more convenient, call waiting is impolite to everyone you're talking to. It is the mechanical version of looking past the person you are with to see if someone more interesting has come into the room. Only call waiting is even worse than that—it always *assumes* that the next person, the person who is calling in, is more interesting than the person you're already speaking to.

At 50—you hate to admit this—you sort of miss the busy signal.

You sense that even the projectionists at movie theaters are always moving around.

In the multiplexes, they have to—with all those screens, all those flickering images in front of all those separate audiences, the projectionists, you envision, are hurrying from compartment to compartment, trying to make sure that all the reels are running in focus and in proper order in all the rooms. The old stereotype of the movie projectionist—dozing in his lair high above the theater, sitting through the featured attraction again and again and again—is gone. Replaced by these guys as frantic as Lucille Ball in the episode about the candy on the conveyor belt.

And if logic tells you that, when a person is always moving, thinking of the next place instead of the place he already is, he may tend to become distracted and fretful and too busy to pay attention to where he is right now . . .

Well, the movie projectionists have that in common with the rest of us—all of us who seem to have forgotten how to stay in one place.

All of the frenzied excitement over the new technology—people rushing to get linked to the various computer networks, to learn the ins and outs of the just-released software programs, to memorize the passwords and initialized commands that will guide them through the maze of solid-state-and-micro-byted communications highways and byways—sometimes strikes you as daunting. By being slow on the uptake with this, are you destined to be falling behind? With every day you fail to familiarize yourself with the new techniques, is your chance of ever catching up fading into the distance?

Relax. Because the most amusing part of the new technology is that it is soon enough going to seem very old. What appears so dazzling and cutting-edge today will, before long, seem archaic and ho-hum. Will seem, in relation to what will soon enough be out there, like movable type does in relation to today's computer universe.

Meaning that there's no rush to learn the new stuff by sundown tonight. Because twenty or thirty years from now, we'll just have to learn newer new stuff all over again. Or at least someone will.

So exhale. Calm down. Log off. Read a book.

Oh. That's right. You already are.

Even while you're noticing that the world can't seem to stop moving around, you acknowledge that this hyperkineticism doesn't apply to you anywhere near as much as it does to those who are younger.

It's one more function of being 50. Whatever urges there are to pick up roots and move on, you've got a million built-in excuses not to. You're settled in at your house, you know your town and your neighborhood, it's hard at your age to imagine another job coming along that will offer something significantly better to make you go through that kind of upheaval . . .

All of which makes sense. The decisions you made when you were young—personal decisions, career decisions, geographic decisions—have hardened up on you. They may have seemed like whims then, but they have turned out to be as irrevocable as the Magna Carta.

So you accept that you are set in your ways now. Sometimes, though, you think back twenty or twenty-five years, and if your memory is correct, you were more than a little set in your ways *then,* too.

When you didn't have to be.

The goal for a lot of people used to be a New York address. It represented the pinnacle—if a business operated out of New York, then that said something about the company's scope, its resources, its influence.

If, someday in the future, that assumption disappears—and it has already started; the grandeur of New York already has diminished considerably—the leading factor responsible for the reversal may turn out to be the 1-800 number. It's one of those changes that have occurred quietly in our adult lifetimes—it wasn't there when we entered the business world, and now it's taken for granted, and its effect has gone far beyond the fact that the phone calls are toll-free. Because today you can set up a business in the smallest town—in Minnesota or Wisconsin or South Dakota—and still have the power of an address on Park Avenue or 57th Street in Manhattan. The 1-800 number, in ways that no one could have foreseen, got rid of the need to make it to the biggest cities. A 1-800 number makes any business national—in a way, makes any business seem bigger than if the business were located in New York or Chicago or Los Angeles.

For men and women who are 50, it can be a difficult concept to get used to—the concept that 1-800 has superseded the concept of place. What 1-800 has done is to announce that there is, in effect, no *place*—place is wherever you decree it to be. *"He's really going places!"*—that phrase that has already changed its meaning for you—becomes further watered down with the new knowledge that wherever the mythical he or she is going, he or she doesn't really

need to make the arduous trip. When you were young, skip-
ping the trip was not an option.

Although, for your parents' generation, it was. What
changed that was an innovation enthusiastically promoted
by the great hero of their time—Dwight Eisenhower. Its
results have probably been something he did not intend.

Eisenhower was the most vociferous proponent of the interstate highway system. He wanted it built—or so he said—
to enable the United States to have uncluttered, high-speed
roadways for the military to use in the event of a future war.
Civilian use of the interstates was seen as an ancillary—a
helpful one, but not the main reason for the highways' existence.

And so they were built. Before they were, for your parents
and your grandparents a trip—even a trip within their own
state, to visit a relative a few hundred miles away—was
something to be undertaken only after a certain amount of
planning and consideration. America in the days before the
interstate highway system was a country of localities and
hometowns whose boundaries might as well have been actual walls—you didn't take off frivolously, even temporarily,
because taking off from your town entailed some doing. To
get there from here was never easy.

For us, it always has been easy—the interstates made taking a trip of many miles as impulsive a decision as picking
up a cheeseburger at a McDonald's drive-through. The concept of distance changed drastically—a journey that to our
parents was a subject to be discussed and debated and,
many times, put off for another year became to us something to do on a restless weekend. The symbolism of getting
out of town was turned completely upside down. City limits
became, seemingly overnight, not limiting at all; the outside world went from being intimidating and foreign and a

little scary to being no big deal. Something to be sampled at will.

The invisible walls of America's hometowns came down; the effect of this on U.S. citizens was arguably much greater than the real tearing down, years later, of the Berlin Wall, but because the interstates happened gradually, mile by mile, county by county, no one made much noise about how those highways would eventually alter everything.

But they have. They never were utilized in precisely the way Eisenhower had envisioned them. But at 50, when you think about how the country used to feel, and how it feels now, his advocacy for the interstates may rank right up there with his military triumphs in Europe during World War II as the events that have had the most significant impact on the national life. In Europe, what he did saved freedom; back home, with the launching of the interstates, he put freedom in a more mundane context than we'd ever known it. We are still feeling the aftershocks with every exit ramp we pass.

On a flight from Phoenix to Chicago, I sat next to a man who was an employee of an engineering company. He lived in Arizona, and was involved in a project that was putting a complicated new sorting system in the Chicago post office. He had worked out a deal where his company would fly him to Chicago once every two weeks for the duration of the long project, put him up in a hotel—and would fly him back home every other weekend so that he could sleep in his own house.

I said that he must have accumulated a lot of frequent-flier miles during the length of the project.

"I have," he said.

I asked him what he was going to do with all the miles; where did he plan to go?

"I don't want to go anywhere," he said. "I'm at the point in my life where the best thing I could hear would be that if I would cash all my frequent-flier miles in, the prize would be that I wouldn't have to go anywhere. The reward would be that I would get to stay home. Isn't that odd?"

I said that it wasn't.

A lifelong resident of New York City, trying to explain to a Midwesterner what it is that makes Manhattan the center of the universe, said, "It's the only place in the world where you can go out at 4 A.M. and get a pastrami sandwich."

Perhaps that's true—but by all accounts not many New Yorkers are leaving their homes willingly at 4 A.M. these days, pastrami sandwich or no. Which may be a parable for all of us, at 50—we who have to de-educate ourselves, to un-teach ourselves the lesson we've been carrying around all of our lives: the lesson that has convinced us that if we don't keep moving every minute of every day, we're missing out on something.

The good, hopeful thing, it is belatedly occurring to us, is to stay in one place. All the travel that we've done, all the locations we've touched down, all the magazines every month offering lists of the "100 best resorts" . . .

And we've finally come to realize that the great challenge is to find one good place—one good place in which to stay put and be happy. Not just a place on a map, but a place inside of us—a place in the heart where all the plans and projects that have never seemed to stop bubbling are at last allowed to take a little rest. A back yard of the soul.

17

The Things You'd Like to Get Back

As you look to the future, there are any number of things you still want to accomplish. But, increasingly, you find that there are also many things you'd like to get back:

I was watching television—one of those magazine-type shows about various aspects of the human drama—and the story was a rather lurid one.

The wife of a prison warden had disappeared with one of the convicts, a man assigned to tend the warden's yard. The story showed the heartbroken warden and his children, and touched on the belief by law-enforcement officials that the wife may have left willingly with the prisoner—that it had been her choice.

There were strong psychosexual undertones to the story, and references to the Stockholm Syndrome, in which hostages fall in love with their captors. Explaining it all to the TV reporter was an FBI agent named Dan Vogel.

Which made sense—we, the public, are not expected to know about the dark underside of life and of human nature, but there are people who are expected to know about it as a part of their jobs, and FBI agents are among those people. So I shouldn't have been surprised to see the FBI man talking about the case.

Except I went to kindergarten with him. Dan Vogel has been a friend of mine since we were 5 years old, playing cowboys and cops-and-robbers. I've always found him to be a very nice person; when my first book was published, Dan was the one and only customer to come to my first book signing. I've tried to keep up with him over the years; on the terrible day of the Oklahoma City bombing, Dan was the FBI spokesman on the scene, and on that day—as on the day I saw him talking about the prison warden's wife—I looked at him on the TV screen and in his face I saw the child I used to know.

At our thirtieth high school reunion, Dan seemed a little sadder, a little more somber, than I had remembered him from the last time we'd talked. He had every right to be; the world is full of awful things, and there are people who are paid to be in the middle of them. From time to time it's good to remember that they all went to kindergarten with someone. And to wish they could somehow get some of that innocence back.

The first time you ever walked into a library, you were filled with sensations so overwhelming that they almost floored you.

The soft quiet, the sweet and clean and dusty library smell, the inviting shadows, and all those rows and rows of books, all those tens of thousands of voices just waiting patiently to teach you things, to tell you stories. More books than you would ever, in a lifetime, be able to get through, more voices than you would ever be able to hear, and there they all were, in that one building, waiting for you. For free.

Just you, very small, and all the voices. You would love to find that feeling one more time—the feeling of when you first stepped into that hushed and wondrous building.

The painters would break for lunch.

You'd see it in the neighborhood where you grew up— the painters would be working on a house, and they would stop for a while at noon, sitting on a piece of canvas they'd thrown down on the floor of the people's garage.

They'd eat the sandwiches they'd brought in brown paper bags, laugh and talk to each other and pour salt onto the tomatoes and hard-boiled eggs they'd packed. What a great thing that seemed like to you—people who liked each other's company, who worked together all day and ate together and had a fine and fun time doing it. For a while there, when you were very young, that's what work seemed like to you—the painters enjoying each other's company in the shade at lunchtime.

You sort of wish you'd never found out that work can mean anything else.

I was on the beach on a hot summer day, and a family was walking toward the water. There was the mother, the father, and three children; the older ones looked like they were 10 and 8, and then there was a boy who appeared to be 2 or 3. He was lagging behind his family, and I could see that he was singing.

As the family passed me, I could hear the words to his song:

"Rudolph with your nose so bright, won't you guide my sleigh tonight . . ."

He wasn't self-conscious at all; here it was, summertime, and he was singing it:

"Then all the other reindeer . . ."

Maybe it was because he was having such a good day. Maybe it was because he connects that song with the happiest, best day of the year—and thought such a day, apparently, could be today.

It's something that at 50 you have pretty much decided is not true. And it's something you wish you could get back. That short, shining time in your life when you really do believe in the possibility that every day can feel as nice as Christmas.

There's an old Alfred Hitchcock movie called *Shadow of a Doubt* in which the female lead—Teresa Wright—is in great peril. Hitchcock filmed the scene beautifully; the Teresa Wright character is downtown at night in the small American town where she lives, and she knows she's in trouble; her fear is played out against the background of the carefree and cheerful crowds of men and women who stroll the sidewalks and cross the busy streets, oblivious to what she is facing.

In addition to being a gripping part of the plot, the scene inadvertently illustrates something that was taken as a given then, and no longer is: the existence of the bustling nighttime downtown, the hub of a city, the place where everyone gathers. Downtown—day or night—used to represent the core of civilization, the city's true center. Hitchcock could film his tension-filled scene there because he knew that the contrast—the fright inside Teresa Wright, the jammed nighttime downtown surrounding her—would work with the audience. They knew that downtown—it looked like their downtown.

No more. No movie director would ever ask his audiences to accept the premise of throngs of well-dressed people at night in a safe, clean and civil American downtown. It would seem like science fiction; it would distract from the plot. It's one more thing, at 50, you'd like to get back— downtown at night as a magnet, downtown America as a logical destination after dark.

Children, when they receive their first phone calls, often don't know how to react.

They've been called to the phone before to speak with grandparents; they've listened to their parents talking on the phone. But the day comes when a friend calls them— when the phone rings, and one of their parents answers, and then says to the son or daughter, with a smile: "It's for you."

The sense of surprise in the child—the look in the child's eyes, the sound in the child's voice—is a gift. *For me? Really? What do I do?* And the sound of that high-pitched and tentative: "Hello?"

For a while, they actually know how many phone calls they've received in their lives. You can ask them, and they'll think and say: "Four." And they'll mean it—they will have remembered every call.

It's something to think about the next time you walk into your hotel room, knowing that the red message light will be flashing; the next time you accept as a given that your voicemail machine at work will be full of calls for you after lunch; the next time you open up your phone bill, knowing how long the list of toll calls will probably be.

Because there was a time, long ago, when the big surprise

was that someone—anyone—had called you. When you could count up all the calls you'd ever had.

It's not that you wish to recapture that, specifically; you know such a thing is not possible, and you probably wouldn't even want it. But the feeling behind it—that first-time feeling—is what you'd like to get back. Fewer and fewer things in your life are first-time things anymore. And you are beginning to realize that the first-time feeling is valuable beyond words.

An appellate court in the Midwest, ruling on a point concerning whether metal detectors should be used in a certain school district, wrote with apparent sadness that just because the metal detectors may be necessary in our schools doesn't mean that we should want them.

Judge Warren Wolfson, writing for the court, said, "We long for the time when children did not have to pass through metal detectors on their way to class, when hall monitors were other children, not armed guards, when students dressed for school without worrying about gang colors."

But we do seem to need the metal detectors, and all the rest. The idea of routine electronic frisking for weapons in schools, as repugnant as it is, seems to be the best attempt at a solution we can come up with. We—and the judge—may indeed wish that adding additional student hall monitors could be the way to ensure safety. But that's a dream.

I remember the first time I encountered a metal detector in an airport. It was in 1973, after a series of airplane hijackings, and the government was just beginning to try them out. They were new to everyone in the airport—there was much puzzlement as we lined up to walk through them—

and one of the people in front of me was a man who set off the buzzer.

He was pulled aside. He was questioned. It turned out that he was a person who wore a leg brace—the metal brace was hidden by his pants. So he had to stand there while the security guard checked out his brace. I knew right then that everything was about to change.

The aspirin bottles in drugstores are triple-sealed now—for our security. We need to show identification cards to get into our office buildings now—for security. And although we wish, along with that judge, that the metal detectors in the schools weren't necessary, we allow them and, in fact, depend on them. Judge Wolfson wrote: "We mourn the loss of innocence this case represents."

The judge seemed to realize that the best thing he could give us is something that we already had, and managed to lose.

But he can't get that back for us. No one can.

When, once in a very great while, you get into an elevator to find an elevator operator running it, you feel that his or her presence is a little intrusive—like someone is watching you.

When you call a business number you're accustomed to calling all the time and are surprised to be answered by a switchboard operator, you occasionally have the feeling—at least fleetingly—that this would be quicker if you could just punch in the extension number like you usually do. And you *hate* automated phone systems—but even you have become trained to depend on them for speed when you're calling businesses where you know the proper extensions.

At 50, you remember when the elevator operators and switchboard operators were common—the standard. The impact of their disappearance—in addition to boosting unemployment figures—is to reduce the bustle-quotient of the American social landscape. Sort of an adjunct to the Hitchcock downtown that's not there any longer. The world without elevator operators and switchboard operators may or may not be more efficient. But it's certainly more sterile. And one more sign, as if you needed one, that you're on your own, in big ways and small.

On summer days with your friends when you were a kid, you all dressed essentially alike. It's not that you planned it—it's just how your world worked back then.

Shorts and T-shirts, with regular shirts worn unbuttoned over them, the long sleeves rolled up; moccasins without socks . . . there was that unspoken feeling that went with the clothes, the signal it sent about friendship and July and being young.

You're tempted to say with a small laugh that you wish your world were still one in which you dressed like your friends. But then you realize that you do—or if not like your friends, then at least like the people you work with every day. Which, at 50, often has to serve as a pale substitute for friendship.

But the feeling's gone. The way you and your colleagues at the office dress sends no signal at all, nor should it. One more thing you'd like to get back, this July or any July at all.

Along with the smallest pleasures that went with those long-ago Julys. Like the many and varied sensations of collecting bottle caps.

The faded colors of the caps, the scratchy surfaces where an opener had pried them off the tops of glass bottles of soda pop, the dozens of brands you knew by the sight of those caps. Some of the brands local, some national . . . collecting those caps and storing them in a cigar box made you feel as if you'd been many places, even if you'd been none.

The smell of those caps—that sweet metallic smell. Gone.

I passed by two businessmen who were walking down the street and I heard one of them say to the other, "Well, I'll do it in March and April, because those two months are slow."

And his colleague nodded, agreeing.

They've got the patterns of the years routinized. They've been through the seasons of their work world so many times that they know this in advance, as a fact: March and April are slow.

If only they—and we, in our own ways—didn't know that. If only we didn't assume that we knew what lay ahead, knew what would be prosperous, knew what would be fallow. The worst part was, I sensed that the two men were probably correct. March and April probably would be slow this year, and the next, and the next. They knew their territory, the territory of their working lives—they were undoubtedly right.

For all the good it would do them.

It's not that you'd literally like to have S&H Green Stamps back. As you recall, they were unwieldy and they stuck together and never quite got pasted into the little Green Stamps redemption booklets the way they were intended to. If your mother ever got around to cashing them in for that steam iron in the prize book, you don't remember it.

But there was something about the idea behind them—the idea that grocers valued your business so much that they'd give you things just for coming in. Maybe it was all a gimmick—maybe the price of the S&H Green Stamps was added onto the price of the groceries.

It seemed like a nice gesture, though—not only was the customer always right, the customer was sincerely wanted. Today, even most bakeries don't believe in baker's dozens—when you order twelve doughnuts or dinner rolls, you get twelve, not thirteen. And no Green Stamps to go with them, in our new and downsized America, land of no bonuses.

You know doctors—friends of yours, people you have met on airplanes or on vacations—who, when they're relaxed, tell you how disillusioned they are about their profession. How it's changed so much from what it was when they first dreamed of becoming physicians.

You wish they could get that Dr. Kildare/Ben Casey dream back, for their sake.

But for your own sake, you wish you didn't know how torn they were about their work. A doctor was supposed to be the guy with the round silver thing strapped to his forehead, the guy who had all the answers, who (everyone assumed) was rich and who took every Wednesday off.

You don't want to know that they have troubles. You certainly believe it when they tell you that the troubles are true, but at 50 you really wish you didn't know.

Bankers, too.

You felt better about the place where you kept your money when you sensed your banker wasn't so nervous for his job. Your banker was supposed to be more solid than you—he, and his bank. So solid that he, and it, got to observe banker's hours. Now when you talk to him he seems always to be asking if you've heard of any good jobs out there. This does not fill you with confidence.

• • •

White T-shirts.

Plain white T-shirts.

Today walk down any city street, stroll through any fairgrounds, and you can find just about any message the human mind can devise, all printed on the fronts and backs of T-shirts. Funny messages, obscene messages, silly messages, bellicose messages; messages promoting sporting-goods companies, messages promoting brands of malt liquor, messages promoting athletic teams, messages promoting the alleged sexual prowess of the shirt-wearer.

What you seldom see—what is shocking when you see it—is a plain white T-shirt.

You'd sort of like to get that back, too. Not that at 50 you usually go around wearing T-shirts. But the days of plain white T-shirts were days when we assumed that the message was us—that whatever was special, or worth noticing, about us was inside the T-shirt, not on the front of it. When the shirts didn't announce who we were—we did.

Or at least we tried to.

There was a moment when you were a child—if you were very lucky:

You'd been away by yourself for the first time, to summer camp. The six weeks were over, and now you were coming back to the town where you lived, and as your family drove up your block with you in the car you could see that there was something tacked to the tree in your front yard.

As the car got closer you could see it was a sign—a sign your family had drawn, welcoming you home. You walked into the house—you didn't want to betray your emotions by running—and everything that happened in the next few minutes felt like a gift. Tiny things—the feel of pulling a glass out of the cupboard and pouring it full of water in the sink of your kitchen, the feel of the banister under your hand as you walked up the stairs to your room—things you had never thought much about, and now you realized, maybe for the first time, how much they represented the meaning of home. You were home, and all of this—your family, all of these sensations—all of this was waiting for you.

At 50, you know there's no chance you'll ever get that back. Not that exactly. But you'd settle for something close.

When we would go to the movies when we were teenagers, it was at the very end of the ornate-movie-palace era (the big downtown movie house in my town was, in fact, called the RKO Palace). When our parents had gone to those downtown movies in the 1930s and 1940s, it had always been a coat-and-tie, nice-dress night out. By the time it was our turn, we were in the most casual of clothes—we were kids in jeans and sneakers in peeling-walled shrines built to hold two or three thousand patrons.

The walls, peeling or not, have been moved in now, in every sense. From those downtown palaces the shrinkage has been relentless: first to smaller theaters in the suburbs, then to chopped-up mall multiplexes off freeway exits, then to video stores, soon to movies-on-demand over phone lines at home.

It's more convenient this way. And, at 50, it doesn't affect us all that much; truth be told, we're just as happy to watch a movie at home. But as we willingly enter this new and smaller world, what of the coming generations who will never know that special feeling—going to the movies with thousands of other people, dressing up for the movies not because you have to but because you want to, looking forward to a night downtown at the movies as a lovely facet of civilized living—of polite society?

• • •

You smile at the memory of those advertisements asking if you were living in an "underphoned home."

And at the memory of the question mark in your mind. Golly—Is our home, indeed, underphoned? Is it possible we have made that mistake?

As if, today, any home could be underphoned. You've got a phone in your car, a phone in your pocket, a phone everywhere you glance. Your many phones give you no chance for peace. Actually, right about now an underphoned home sounds pretty good.

Although if you were to decide today that your home was underphoned, you could not only not assume that "a man from the phone company" would come out to remedy the situation. At 50, you have to confess that you don't even really know which "phone company" is the phone company.

You'd like to go into a hobby shop. To walk among the model planes, tasting the smell of the airplane glue, the plastic parts, the feel of the slippery decals. To savor the prospect of two or three days of you and the model-airplane kit and the silence and fun of doing something by yourself and actually getting it done and having it be good.

You'd like—half a century on—to find a place where you could go to buy that.

Our full-color world of videotape—so realistic and sharply defined, the colors rich and deep and bright—has certain inadvertent drawbacks.

Epitomized by this:

No golfer dressed in gaudy colors, regardless of how skilled he is, will ever have the visceral impact on the country of the young Arnold Palmer, televised in black and white, walking up a fairway, squinting, hitching up his pants as he strode toward the black-and-white green.

You now understand, at 50, that there was something about black-and-white television—something about the implied distance that it represented, about the difference between those black-and-white TV images we saw, and the full-color lives that we led—that almost inexplicably made everything in black and white seem bigger, that gave those things we saw an aura of scale and even of nascent history. A sense that the literal full-color video world somehow does not confer.

At 50, you are tireder than you used to be. You are older than you used to be. You have nothing—or very little—to stay up late at night for.

So—this question keeps coming up—why can't you sleep through the night?

Sleeping through the night, at 50, would seem like something that would be so easy for you. Sleeping through the night, for the weary, 50-year-old person you are, would seem to be your best event.

But you are becoming like an infant who, no matter when he or she goes to sleep, will be up in a few hours. If you go to bed at 10 P.M., you're just about certain that you will find yourself wide-awake and staring at that clock at 1:30 A.M. Or 3:30 A.M. Or (and?) 5:30 A.M.

Why? Not because there's anything in particular on your mind. That's the most maddening part—it's not that you wake up in the middle of the night for any good reason. You wake up because . . .

Well, you don't know what the reason is. But those middle-of-the-night digits on the clock are becoming familiar and trustworthy friends. You can count on them being there, just about every night.

•   •   •

And:

When you were 15, you could sleep until 10 A.M., easily. Ten o'clock in the morning seemed to be a pretty reasonable time to be waking up.

Today if someone offered you a million dollars in cash, you couldn't will yourself to sleep all the way until 10 A.M.

You would like to get back the feeling of joy and surprise that washed over you as a child when you looked out the window to see that your dad was lugging home a big new bag of sand to put in the sandbox for your brother and sister and you. Such a humble present—that sand clean and soft and white—but few gifts you have received since have caused in you the sense of gratitude and delight. Perhaps because it represented someone thinking about you, and noticing that there was something in your world that needed fixing and replenishing, and taking care of it without you asking. What a sight—your dad hauling that bag out of the car and toward the back yard. His reward being the look in your eyes.

All the carefully planned itineraries of your life at 50, all the vacation trips to exotic destinations, all the attempts to provide yourself with a rewarding and pleasurable break from your routine . . .

Yet have any of these attempts to reward yourself ever felt as enticing as the beginning of a summer night when you were young, pulling into the gas station with your friends and asking for fifty cents' worth of regular to get the evening started?

You didn't know where you were going, other than that you weren't going far. But at 50, given everything else, you'd like to be out tonight with the best friends you had when you first had best friends. This has nothing, or at least little, to do with your degree of satisfaction with the life you're living now. Yet everything else being equal, when the sun goes down today you'd like to be in that car with them, waiting for the gas to be pumped in, getting ready for a hometown evening, one evening in a succession of evenings that, at one point in your life, you thought would never end.

That's what you'd like to get back—something so simple, something there's no retrieving.

18

"Who Moved That Lamp?": The New, Cranky You

The sweet, ethereal dreaminess of those things you'd like to get back is pleasant to bask in—part illusion, all joy.

But the cold fact is, you're becoming crotchety. And although you don't like to dwell on it, the things that set you off range from the tiny to the significant. You encounter them daily.

None more so than your utter conviction that the world is not sufficiently quiet.

The street outside your house. The lobby of the bank. The corridor that runs by your office at work. You are always shooting dark glances at the noises you hear.

On a universal scale, you are your father, constantly muttering, "Turn that damn music down."

• • •

Not that you are unaware that this is occurring. You don't want to be this cranky. It is happening to you against your will.

You can feel it sneaking up on you every time—you tell yourself, "Oops, here it comes." At a restaurant the soup arrives too soon; the soup arrives too late. The waiter asks you for your dinner selection before you've had a chance to look at the menu; the waiter is nowhere to be found when you're ready. You know that this is no one's fault but your own; you have reached the point in your life, you reluctantly admit, when no one can do anything right.

And when did order become so important to you?

As in, who moved that chair over there?

Or: That lamp by the window—is it a few inches out of place?

At 50, your eye for these kinds of things is becoming a little too sharp. There doesn't seem to be a thing you can do to stop it.

All of which makes you understand, for the first time, why your parents don't seem all that thrilled when you—a grown adult—come into their house and immediately turn the air conditioner up, or turn the heat down.

You do this because you've always thought of your parents' house as your house—that's the way it was from the day you were first old enough to remember things. In your mind, you have always belonged in their house, long after you moved out on your own.

So of course you hit that air-conditioning lever. Of course you adjust the thermostat down. Why wouldn't you?

The reason you wouldn't—or at least shouldn't—is that it's not your house. It's their house. So when you breeze in and start fooling with the temperature controls without asking them, you shouldn't be surprised that they seem just a bit annoyed.

Because you can see it coming in your own life. You look around your house and you try to imagine someone, even a family member, coming in and messing around with the little things. You don't like the thought. It's your house. You like it the way it is.

The same way your parents like theirs.

You didn't used to mind sitting through the movie previews and the cartoons. In fact, it was kind of fun.

At 50, you often take it as a personal offense. You—the new, cantankerous you—have paid good money to be in this theater, you have arrived on schedule—and now they're wasting your time, showing endless advertisements and other things you have no desire to see. You're here for the movie you have chosen to view—why are they trifling with you like this?

(And the very concept of a movie theater—sitting in a dark room full of total strangers—strikes you anew as questionable.)

Stodginess, when it insinuates itself into your life, arrives in precise increments. You don't become stodgy in a broad, general way; it happens bit by bit, day by day.

Thus, you wish someone would do something about those bicycle messengers. Don't they know to watch where they're going?

At 50, you go into the little grocery store and ask the woman behind the counter to give you a container of mixed fruit, and to go heavy on the pineapple. You really want a lot of pineapple in there, you tell her.

To you, you're like an enthusiastic kid showing the person what you want. Nothing wrong with that.

To the woman behind the counter, you're some crotchety 50-year-old, set in your ways. *Make sure you give me enough pineapple.* As if she didn't hear you the first time.

She knows you. They all know you. You're the one who's always telling them to put the extra pineapple in there, even though they're quite aware of what you want.

Two different visions of you:

Yours: the happy, hungry kid going to the grocery store.

Theirs: the demanding crank who doesn't trust anyone else to get anything right.

You're not sure you want to know which vision is the accurate one.

In your local newspaper on the first day of spring, you see a photograph of some boys and girls skateboarding on the steps of the town's department store.

You don't think: Those children look like they're having a good time.

You think: The owner of the department store must really be annoyed. Those kids are making a nuisance of themselves.

You turn the page, looking for something else in the news to upset you.

Waiting in line—any line—is too long.

Lines were always just a part of life—part of what you did during the course of a day, beginning with your first lunches in the elementary school cafeteria. Lines were to be expected.

Today even two people in a line are too many for you.

You realize that this has almost nothing to do with the line, and almost everything to do with you.

• • •

At 50, a detour sign is an inconvenience rather than an opportunity.

Literally—on the highway—and figuratively, in the other parts of your life. Your first response to a detour is to resent it, rather than to welcome the prospect of the unexpected places it might take you—places, were it not for the sign, you would never get a chance to see.

You realize this about yourself even as you curse the detour.

And when people stand too close to you, it sets off signals, as audible to you as if they were sirens.

You ask yourself when this started—these invisible wires that seem to extend from you, monitoring your imagined territory.

"This is like going out to dinner with grandpa."

The person speaking those words was Paul Sullivan, a young sportswriter with whom I was attempting to eat a meal. We were in the same city on assignment, we had met in a restaurant for dinner, and I had commented—after the waiter had brought our drinks and had walked away from the table—that the fellow's fingernails were dirty.

To which Sullivan responded with the grandpa comment.

"How can you say that?" I asked him.

"Because I can't believe that you're complaining about the waiter's fingernails," he said.

"I didn't say it to him," I said. "He didn't hear me. I said it to you."

"Grandpa," he said.

"You don't care that the guy who's bringing you your food has dirty fingernails?" I said.

"I don't spend my time looking at waiters' fingernails," Sullivan said.

"That's exactly my point," I said. "How many restaurant meals have you had in your life? Hundreds? Thousands?"

"What are you trying to say?" Sullivan said.

"Out of all the restaurant meals you've had in your life, how many times have you noticed that the waiter has dirty fingernails?" I said.

"None," Sullivan said.

"Me, either," I said. "Until tonight. I've never thought that a waiter has dirty fingernails before. This is the first time."

"Grandpa," he said.

There was the chance, of course, that we were both right. That I had, indeed, never taken note of a waiter's dirty fingernails before—and that I was acting, in Sullivan's eyes, like a crotchety grandpa. It wasn't a case of every waiter or waitress I had ever encountered having Ivory-clean hands—it was just a case of me crossing that invisible line in a person's life, the line on the other side of which every human contact is an invitation to find something to complain about.

"I looked at the guy's fingernails after you said it, the next time he came back to the table," Sullivan said. "They weren't so bad."

"But they were dirty, right?" I said.

"They probably could have been a little cleaner," Sullivan said.

"See!" I said. "I was right!"

"It was no big deal," he said. "They weren't all that dirty."

I had a feeling that this was merely the first day of my looking-at-the-waiter's-fingernails life. Not the most promising of thoughts.

"Oh, no," I said.

"What?" Sullivan said. *"What?"*

"He just dragged our salads through the tree."

"Who?" Sullivan said. *"What* tree?"

I nodded toward the kitchen. Our waiter, passing one of those long-leafed trees that some restaurants use to decorate their interiors, had carried our salad plates right through the leaves.

"He didn't touch the tree," Sullivan said.

"Look," I said. "He did. The leaves are still moving."

"I can't have any more dinners with you on this trip," Sullivan said.

You almost tell a kid to put out the cigarette, turn his baseball cap around so it faces the right way, and pull up the shorts that are hanging down to his ankles.

You don't even know the kid. You've never seen him before. You've merely noticed him on the street.

Yet you almost say those things.

You're your dad, bawling out . . .

Bawling out who?

You? That kid's not you. He's just some kid you don't know. And you're 50. And cranky.

As much fun as you make of yourself for starting to be this way, sometimes something will happen that makes you think about your apparent inability to stop the steady progression of it.

One evening I was about to watch a basketball game on television—one I really didn't care all that much about. I had bought a submarine sandwich; I put half of it in the oven, heated it up, put it on a plate, pulled a cold can of beer from the refrigerator and sat down in front of the TV set.

The phone rang. It was one of the best friends I've ever had, calling from another city just to talk.

And I felt vaguely annoyed. At him. For interrupting something.

Now, what had he interrupted? The game? The game didn't matter—it was just going to serve as a time killer for me. I didn't have an allegiance to either team.

The meal? I'd already heated the sandwich up once—I could either eat it while I talked to him, or heat it up again once we were finished. And there was another half of the sandwich waiting.

The beer? Plenty more in the icebox—and I could drink it while we talked, anyway.

But on some dumb level, I really was annoyed, because in my head I'd planned the evening—ball game, sub sandwich, beer—and my friend had disrupted it. This made absolutely no sense at all—this twinge of irritation. I should have been grateful and happy to hear from my friend.

But—like someone who resents it when that thermostat is readjusted without anyone asking him, like someone who doesn't want anyone else moving that favorite chair of his even a couple of inches—I sat there feeling that certain small degree of annoyance. I had no schedule for the evening—whatever schedule I was thinking he'd thrown off course didn't even exist.

And it made me imagine what was to come in the years ahead. Because this time, I could tell my friend about what I was thinking, and we could laugh about it. How stupid it was.

Later, though . . . years from now . . .

Later maybe something like this happens and you don't even laugh about it. Later, years from now, maybe something like this happens and you get upset about it and you don't know to think that it's funny. Because to you, it's not. You're stuck in your ways, and it's not a joke.

You call City Hall in the town where you live and you tell them that they really should put a stoplight up at the corner of Powell and Ardmore.

And after you've hung up the phone you realize that you've become proprietary about the town. You at last have reached that point where you no longer feel it's someone else's town, the town of all the people who were there before you were born; you've reached the point at which you think it's yours, and that you should be calling the shots.

That corner's getting too busy to have no stoplight. Doesn't anyone know that?

So you call City Hall. Like you're ordering a new garden hose or bathroom fixtures. Put the stoplight up, you tell them. You have been walking past that corner for almost half a century.

You notice something about married couples who are older than you are—people of your parents' generation, parents of the people you grew up with.

If they want to make plans with their friends—people their same age—and their friends can't do it, they occasionally tend to act a little hurt.

As if it's an insult. As if their friends' unavailability is a personal comment about them, and not just a scheduling conflict.

You find yourself thinking about whether this is another one of the non-funny aspects of getting older—whether the impulse to read something personal into things like this inevitably comes with the territory of being old. Because you know that earlier in the adult lives of a man and a woman—when they are in their 20s or 30s—if their friends are committed to doing something else on a Saturday night, they usually shrug it off without much of a thought. It doesn't mean anything.

Apparently, as men and women grow older, it does mean something. At least it is perceived as meaning something— as a measure of acceptance or rejection that to you seems out of line with the reality of the situation. You, even at 50, don't quite understand all this. But you have seen it enough to know that as people get ever older, everything evidently grows in significance. Even a "We're sorry, but we have plans that night."

"I think this is Broadway coming up," I said.

It wasn't.

"This may be Broadway here," I said.

It wasn't.

"Slow down," I said. "This has to be Broadway."

It wasn't.

I turned to the person who was driving—Paul Sullivan again, the young sportswriter who thought I was grandpa at the dinner table. We were trying to find a side street. I told him I was getting worried that we might have missed it.

I said:

"It was supposed to be a mile past that last stoplight, and it's been more than a . . ."

"Will you shut up?" he said.

"I just think we've passed Broadway," I said.

"I've looked at every street sign," he said. "We have not passed Broadway. You are so high-maintenance."

Meaning a bother. Meaning crotchety.

Now . . . in my own mind I wasn't being high-maintenance. I was still the same way I was when I was first driving around in cars with my friends—always sure we're going to miss the exit, always checking to make certain that we're going the right way. Whatever my idiosyncrasies are, they are lifelong idiosyncrasies. Nothing new.

Except that, at 50, the things that didn't mean anything much to anyone when you were younger all of a sudden help to classify you as grumpy, a grouch. You add the 50 factor to the quirks you've always had, and people begin to see you as W. C. Fields.

"I'm not high-maintenance," I said to Sullivan. "How can you say that?"

He took a hard right turn.

"Where are you going?" I said.

"This is Broadway," he said.

At 50 it drives your blood pressure up when you go to a store to buy a nice outdoor jacket—just a regular, single-color outdoor jacket—and you find that there are no jackets for sale that don't have rings or swirls or multi-hued stars or amoebas on them. If you buy a jacket, you have to be resigned to leaving the store looking like an Olympics logo.

Looking like you're trying out for something. At 50, you don't want to try out for anything. You just want a jacket. No wonder you're frowning in the checkout aisle.

You are suspicious of the new neighbors.

Any new neighbors.

You think that they may disrupt things. That they may be too noisy, or run their sprinkler too long, or play their music too high-volume. That they may let their lawn sprout weeds, or bang their car doors late at night, or let their kids have beer parties.

You have every potential of becoming the grumpy next-door neighbor.

You actually forget some of the neighbors you've had during your life.

You've had so many.

19

Looking Toward a Future Without Mount Rushmore

When you consider the future, there are things that will make you laugh; there are things that will make you feel glum; there are things that will make you sit and think.

Your best bet, of course, is to choose to laugh about the things that have the potential to make you cry. Although when it comes to this particular subject—the subject of some of the darker precincts that lie ahead—if you are honest with yourself you will concede that laughter can be a continuing challenge.

However, our shared reluctance notwithstanding, these matters do require addressing:

For starters, you begin to come to terms with the fact that we're all just passing through.

On the largest of levels, for example, you're pretty sure that you are never going to end up on the side of Mount

Rushmore. That possibility you can with some confidence discard.

But, two years after you retire, will you be remembered at your office? Will they ever talk about you—will your name come up in conversation?

It's something you have no control over, and you accept that. Yet not being able to do anything about it doesn't mean you have to like it.

When you were a kid in school, you and your friends may have painted your initials on the railroad overpass in your town; it was your first attempt to try to assure yourself a lasting presence in a place that mattered to you. But when you came home from college for vacation your freshman year, some other group of kids had painted their initials over yours. It's the way of the world.

And at 50, you are aware that whatever lasting presence you are trying to forge, someone will soon enough come along with their own can of paint. The same way you did—not looking back.

When you are a young adult, you really want your city to sit up and take notice of you.

Now you understand that cities can't take note of anything. They're not thinking entities. No one can "conquer" a city, because a city doesn't know or remember anything. Your city was here before you, it will be here after you; it doesn't know anyone.

It's like that idea of going to Paris or Africa someday—that idea that if you do, you do, but if you don't, Paris will have no idea you were never there. It's not waiting for you, no matter how you may want to fool yourself into thinking it is.

And the way to leaven these kinds of thoughts is to realize that we are all temps.

From the CEO of General Motors to the person who is literally working as a temp in the GM clerical pool, the truth that we all must eventually come to accept is that all work is temporary work—that we're all merely sitting in for a while.

For the well-being of the American workplace, it's essential that people don't come to this understanding too soon. But by 50, it's beginning to set in: All the striving, all the plotting, all the planning—and the world, it turns out, is a temporary-placement agency.

A lot of men, once they pass 50, start to think that they want to have formal portraits taken.

The kind you see on the walls of corporate boardrooms; the kind in which business executives sit in dark suits with their hands folded on their laps, their smiles faint. Sometimes with a globe in the foreground of the picture.

These are posterity pictures—pictures showing their subjects as serious people striking serious poses. The people in the pictures may, like us, have silently concluded that Mount Rushmore is not going to happen. But these portraits are their personal versions of it; these portraits will have to do.

Some year down the line, you may find yourself tempted to sit for one of these portraits. Go ahead.

But after the session, go out and do something enjoyable and stupid. The picture will be waiting for you in the morning. Somber and sober.

Bricks in the plazas.

You're noticing them already. It's a fairly new notion—communities and schools raising money by selling the bricks for $50 or $100, with the name of the donor carved into the face of the brick.

The idea is to construct public plazas with those bricks, for future generations to walk upon. Sort of like the palm prints on the sidewalk in front of Grauman's Chinese Theater in Hollywood, but available to anyone. They're even doing it at Disney World—your family can purchase a brick to be placed on a walkway near the Magic Kingdom, so your names will be there forever.

Out of nowhere, this desire for immortality is beginning to make itself felt. It appears to be what we want. All those years of assuming that nothing that happens after we're gone will have any effect on us—and here come the bricks in the plazas.

Some of which must stem from a growing sense that not all of the things on the list will ever get done.

The list may not be a literal list, but you've been carrying it around with you for most of your life. There may be books you've promised yourself to write, houses you've vowed to construct, canvases you've told yourself you'd paint, trips you've planned to take.

And for the first time, you begin to come to the studied conclusion that they're not all going to happen. That perhaps you'd better start thinking about shortening the list, editing it—making sure it's not cluttered with unnecessary items that will get in the way of the important ones.

What a thought, when you picture your future—the thought that there will be items left over at the end, items on your list you never quite get to. The list never bore any sense of urgency before. You just kept adding on to it, knowing you'd have time to get to all of it later.

That's what you thought you knew.

If there's a certain reluctance at 50 to spend too much energy looking too far ahead, it is with good reason.

This can be summed up, at least symbolically, in seven words.

Some older people I know—the man in his 80s, the woman in her 70s—went South to spend the winter, and before they departed on the trip they expressed concern about the logistics. All the luggage to be transported from their home in the North to the distant condominium—at their age they weren't sure about how they were going to deal with it.

After they had arrived, though, they said to their friends, with a note of some satisfaction:

"We didn't have to touch a bag."

They had taken care to line up in advance enough help from people along the way—at home, at the two airports, at the condominium complex—that from the time they walked out the door of their house to the time they settled in for the long vacation, they hadn't had to lug the stuff around. Those seven words: "We didn't have to touch a bag."

Which was nice.

But if that's what victory is going to consist of in our not-all-that-distant futures—if not having to touch a bag is, genuinely, going to stand as a note of triumph—then that's probably a good enough reason for us not to spend too much time gazing relentlessly into crystal balls. Because whether or not we endeavor to figure out what awaits us, it's going to be waiting for us anyway.

Hopefully with someone to carry it upstairs.

I was out for a walk one night and I looked up at the moon and I thought about the people I had met who had walked upon its surface.

Two of them, if I remembered correctly; maybe three. Only twelve people in the history of the world have walked on the moon; because of the nature of the business in which I work, I've had the opportunity to spend time talking with some of them, and as I walked down a Midwestern sidewalk on that recent night I looked at the moon and it all seemed impossible.

Whatever the future will feel like, it probably will not include this—will not include knowing men and women from our own planet who have walked upon the moon. That realization again: What we could do then, we can't do now.

The future was always the moon. It seemed so odd to walk along the sidewalk and look up—to think about the twelve—and to realize that the moon is now the past.

An army buddy from World War II called my father. The man had some trouble reaching him; the phone number my father had given him to call was off by one digit. The man had to do some checking before he got the right number.

"It was my fault," my father said. "I'm starting to make mistakes."

As matter-of-fact as that. I don't know whether he accepts it as easily as he said it: "I'm starting to make mistakes." But it's something that all of us are going to have to think about—something we can't plan for and can't avoid and, by all indications, something we won't be able to do much to change. But we can look the people we love in the eyes, and we can tell them. Which will never be a mistake.

On a much lighter note—and we're going to need all the much lighter notes we can get:

Will we fall prey to the smiley-face compulsion?

For years, we have been opening letters sent by older relatives, and inside the letters are clippings from newspapers, or sometimes cartoons. They've been cut out and mailed to us because the older relative thought we'd get a kick out of them. And—on the clipping, on the cartoon— the relative will have drawn a smiley face.

No words; no message—unless you count the smiley face as a message, which you probably should. The smiley face means: Hope you laugh at this. It means: Here's a shared joke that both of us understand.

You see these smiley-face-festooned clippings on the fronts of refrigerators all over the country. The smiley-face clippings are never sent by younger friends or relatives— they always come from someone older.

And the question is: Does the future hold this in store for us, too? Will we, on some pre-set day on the inner calendar of our lives, begin tearing stories out of magazines, drawing smiley faces on them, and mailing them off to young relatives? Is it an unavoidable part of the aging process?

Please let it be avoidable.

The people to give a wide berth in the years to come will be the people who were never famous before 50, but who will become very famous after 50.

It will happen—always through television, often through commercials these people star in for the companies they own. This first-time fame can be an awful thing to observe. Men and women who have been famous for all of their adult lives—movie stars, athletes, TV performers—tend to soften their edges by the time they're 50. They're accustomed to the fame, and to all the absurdities that come with it. They can smile at it (although not draw smiley faces on it).

But the ones who never knew what fame felt like until they are past 50—watch out. They're the ones who become

drunk with it. They're the ones who go nuts. You'll see. It
happens every generation.

Not that it matters—we'll be gone—but the way we'll be
seen by generations who come along well after ours is a
humbling thing to consider.

"Seen" in the literal sense. Think of the old newsreel
footage of Babe Ruth and Herbert Hoover. Or Woodrow
Wilson, waving stiffly, wearing a straw hat. Now, you can
assume that the Babe and Hoover and Wilson undoubtedly
thought they looked pretty regular in those moving pictures—that they looked all right. Yet to us they look like
something as antiquated as if their likenesses had been un-
earthed from the ruins of Peloponnesus.

Part of this is because of the technology—the herky-jerky
effect caused by the old black-and-white movie film and the
way it recorded pictures. But even if the turn-of-the-century
men and women had somehow been recorded on our modern video cameras, you suspect that they would look like a
separate species.

Which means only one thing: We will, too.

We may think, at a Memorial Day picnic or a Thanksgiv-
ing dinner, that we present a visual image so contemporary
and so thoroughly evolved that nothing in the future could
ever make us look out of date.

But count on it: Sixty or eighty or a hundred years from
now, people will be looking at those videotapes of us and
thinking we're as odd as Warren G. Harding or Christy
Mathewson.

The Exclusion Principle's going to get us.

If you want to know what it's going to feel like, then just
consider what goes through the minds of our parents' generation when they see a television commercial for breakfast

cereal set to the background music of James Brown singing "I Feel Good." Or a commercial for a long-distance phone company set to the tune of a Beatles sound-alike group singing "Help!"

Songs and singers that were regarded as societal threats when the songs and singers first came along—when we were children—are now so mainstream that the biggest corporations use them to move the merchandise. We all know that.

What we haven't thought much about yet, though, is that when we get to be the age our parents are now, songs that haven't even been written today, sung in styles that have not yet been heard, will be played in television commercials in an effort to get men and women much younger than us to reminisce and feel warm and tingly. The songs—songs that today, this very morning, don't even exist—will be oldies, lures to get American adults to dream about their youth.

Adults who will be nowhere near as old as we will be— adults whose oldies will have the power to move them to tears, and will draw a total blank in us. Is our parents' generation just the slightest bit resentful, being asked to purchase products to the tunes of the Rolling Stones and the Monkees?

Wouldn't you be resentful—being left out of the nation's nostalgia?

You will be, soon enough.

Also:

As boring as you think "Volare" is when played at a piano bar, some kid who's now 6 years old will feel the same way about "Stairway to Heaven" at some piano bar in the year 2042.

• • •

On the days you feel especially enslaved to your voice mail—when you wish that just once you'd return from lunch and find that no one had called—don't be too fervent in those hopes.

Chances are, they'll come true.

So many businesspeople—influential, busy, in control—go through their careers with the phone ringing constantly. Ringing so much that they begin to hate the sound of the ring.

And then they retire.

Many of them announce that they are going to become "consultants"—which usually means that they have business cards printed up and a phone put into an office in a converted room at home. And the phone sits silent; the answering machine is always empty. They may put in a dedicated fax line, only to find that there's seldom a fax.

It doesn't always work out that way. But we've all seen it happen to some of the people who were the most dynamic and driven in our offices. So next time your voice-mail load threatens to overwhelm you:

Enjoy it. Believe it or not, you may miss it someday.

One of these days you'll see a person crossing the street and you'll be sure that he's someone who sat next to you in the third grade.

And then it will occur to you that the person is an old man. Just one more thrill that the future holds: An old man will look like a third grader to you.

Speaking of which:

If you happen to live in the same community where you grew up, there is a very good chance that some of the friends with whom you went to kindergarten will end up living with you in the retirement community, senior citizens' residence, or nursing home that will be your last mailing address.

On the one hand, it's sort of reassuring. At least you'll know some of these people—you won't be among strangers.

But of course it's also too dismal to think about: the kid you played kickball with at recess sharing the table with you in the communal dining hall at Shady Acres.

That one phrase—"nursing home"—is, for obvious reasons, one you don't even like to hear. You're only 50, after all—looking into the future is one thing, but there's no need to be obsessively gloomy about it.

But here's a thought:

There's probably political infighting for the corner room at the nursing home.

You think not? Ambition and avarice don't suddenly disappear just because a person turns 80 or 90. You watch—you'll get there, which will be depressing enough, only to find that someone's trying to ace you out of the room with the nicest view.

As long as we're on the dreaded subject:

If you, at 50, can't count on the waitress to get your order right; if you can't count on the delivery man to bring your merchandise on the day he was supposed to; if you can't count on the clerk at the hotel's front desk to give you the correct version of the message you've been waiting for . . .

Then what makes you think that, thirty or forty years down the line, you're going to be able to count on the people who work in the nursing home to treat you right?

Don't let the thought ruin your day.

• • •

There will always be someone to turn a profit from what seems to be bad news.

The first person to market the concept of funeral tapes, for example, will make himself a billionaire. It's surprising that no one has thought of it yet.

Funerals—listen, you thought this chapter was going to get cheerier after the nursing-home stuff?—have traditionally been dominated by speeches given either by members of the clergy who didn't really know the deceased all that well, or by friends and relatives who do their best to say nice things about the dearly departed, but who aren't experts at expressing their thoughts in public.

So when the generation that is now turning 50 finally breathes its last at some time in the future, the answer to successful funerals will lie in the same medium that has always spoken most eloquently to us: music.

Specifically, the music we've always loved—the music we grew up with. The funeral tapes would be custom-designed—a person would leave detailed instructions about which songs he or she wanted played at his or her funeral, in which order. For instance, a man might choose James Taylor's "Walking on a Country Road" to be played as the congregation files in; the Faces' "Stay with Me" to brighten the atmosphere as the audience waits for the service to begin; the Beatles' "We Can Work It Out" as the people sit in silent contemplation; and the Beach Boys' "Good Vibrations" to send everyone out to the street in a mellow mood, feeling warm thoughts about the person who was their reason for being here on this day.

People make customized tapes for their listening pleasure in their cars—so what would be so wrong with funeral tapes? The music available to put on the tapes—the music of the last forty years—certainly is more evocative to this generation than the usual funeral dirges are. And by carefully selecting the songs for a funeral tape, a man or a woman would be sending one last message to the people in the pews about what his or her outlook on life was: what was moving, what was lighthearted, what mattered.

All in a language instantly understood by everyone in attendance. Whatever marketer picks up on this idea first will make an absolute fortune.

(Of course, this will also engender intense competition over who has the best funeral.)

I saw a man try to sneak into a half-price event open only to senior citizens. The cutoff age was 55, which I thought was pretty generous—the sponsors could have made it 65. And this guy—I knew this for a fact—was 53.

Yet there he was in line. He saw me looking at him and gave me a grin and a shrug. Like "Hey, what can you do?"

Another man told me that in Florida people sell second-hand handicapped-parking permits at flea markets. Allegedly they go for a good price.

This does not bode well for the future. Are we destined to be surrounded by amoral and larcenous geezers, geezers our age snapping up bogus handicapped stickers, the late-life equivalent of buying Rolling Stones tickets from scalpers outside the stadium?

(Mick Jagger will probably get his handicapped sticker as part of his contract rider.)

Any number of your friends—upon the death of one of their parents—have talked to you about the flood of emotions that washes over them as they clean out their parent's desk drawers and closets.

They always tell you the stories in the same way: "I was cleaning out my dad's desk drawer, and I could hardly go on. The little things reminded me of what I knew about him, and also how much I didn't know . . .''

When you hear that you begin to think about the future, and for some reason you wish that some impersonal workman could clean out your desk drawers and your closets and your basement and toss out the contents without looking at them, like a housekeeper cleans out a hotel room on the morning a guest checks out—that someone could remove every artifact of your life as if you were that hotel guest. So that on the day after you left for good, it would appear that no one was ever there.

You're not sure why you feel that way. But the idea of people—even people who love you—going slowly and carefully through your things in your absence, drawing conclusions about you, reading their own thoughts into your life . . .

Your life, you tell yourself, is your business. Even after you're gone. Except—from everything you hear—this is never so.

But amid the occasional shadows there is also much lightness. One more pressing question about the future:

Those of us turning 50 grew up accepting the idea that the apex of public displays of enthusiasm and approval was the standing ovation. That's how an audience rewarded a person who'd really made it to the top—a standing ovation.

The emerging generation of younger Americans, though, routinely expresses its admiration for the quality of a performance by barking and going "wooo-wooo-wooo." This is standard—if a performer pleases an audience, the automatic reward is the audience members barking like dogs and making that "wooo" sound.

So this gives us something to look forward to. As we grow older—eventually too old to stand up for a standing ovation—we can watch with curiosity what will happen to today's young men and women as they, too, approach 50. Whether they will eventually be like we are, standing and applauding. Or whether they will continue, half a century into their own lives, to bark.

And wooo.

20

Ballparks and Wal-Marts, Rewards and Joys

The rewards—the joys—of 50 can be quiet and low-key and deeply satisfying. There are so many of them. And finding this out—finding out, against all previous expectations, just how much you like being at this particular place—turns out to be the best reward of all.

At 50 entire months go by without you worrying once that maybe there is someone out there who is having a better time than you are tonight.

What a consuming preoccupation that used to be—the thought that somewhere people might be having more fun than you were, that somewhere that party (either literal or metaphorical) really was going on, and that you were compelled to find it.

No more. You now realize that they probably aren't out

there after all—and that even if they are, there's no need for you to find them. You're fine where you are tonight.

Which extends to your newfound prudence about getting too worked up over every new thing that is promoted as being the greatest, the breakthrough, the most revolutionary . . .

You now know that just about everything is derivative. Always has been. Whatever new rock band that is gracing the cover of the latest cutting-edge magazine this month, its members are just walking down the same path that the Beatles and the Rolling Stones walked before them. The sullen new movie actor with the hooded eyelids and the muttered complaints about the existential futility of life is just doing Brando. The blonde sex bomb who is making headlines for the revealing clothes she wears in public places is copying what she learned from Marilyn Monroe and Brigitte Bardot.

All the raucous new television situation comedies that the network publicists work overtime to make you tune in to, to make you think are worth planning your evenings around—they may or may not be funny, but they're in the end merely new attempts to do *The Honeymooners* and *My Three Sons.*

Nothing wrong with any of this; it was ever thus. But at 50 you look behind all the shouting and all the hyperbole about the entertainment that is supposed to excite you, and what you see being turned out is carbon copies of what you've already seen. Sometimes good carbon copies, sometimes not-so-good. But you'll hold your excitement in reserve, if no one minds. Your excitement is still available. It just knows enough now to play hard-to-get.

• • •

There was a time in your life—this makes you smile, at 50—
when you had the absolute need to gain the approval and
respect of anyone who was a year older than you were.

It's hard to remember now—how important it was, when
you were a kid, to impress someone just because the person
happened to be born in the year previous to the year you
were born. How just about anyone a year older than you
had the implicit authority to make you want to gain their
regard.

You look around you now—having little idea who is exactly how old—and you think back with affection and
whimsy to those days when such things mattered so much.

Finally—when there is no one in the world to tell you what
your bedtime is—you are always in bed before bedtime.

The appeal of instant gratification has not entirely gone
away. It has simply changed venues.

So your wanderlust leads you not to places of blaring
music and half-dressed members of the opposite sex and
bottles of exotic alcoholic concoctions, but to the Target
and Wal-Mart stores out by the interstate exit.

All of those aisles stacked with things you didn't even
know you wanted, priced so that you will race toward the
checkout counter with them; all those household items, col-
orful and plentiful, each beckoning to you, each silently
teasing "Why not?" . . .

It's instant gratification, all right, instant gratification at
every turn of the shopping cart in a clean, well-lighted
place that wants you there: at 50, your preferred version of
a honky-tonk dance hall. Sixty-four registers, no waiting.

You begin to realize that the *Reader's Digest* has very interesting articles.

•   •   •

Once in a while, when you are at the supermarket and you are picking up a six-pack of beer, you stop to think that there was a time when this was the most thrilling and illicit thing you could do.

When you were not old enough to do this legally—when you had visions of being given the electric chair if anyone in authority caught you doing this. When you spent hours—days—plotting with your friends about how to accomplish this impossible task.

At 50 you drop the six-pack into the grocery cart, with the cheese and the laundry detergent and the bread. The clerk in Aisle 3 runs your purchases over the computerized scanner, adding up your total without even looking you in the eye.

You leave the store and, just for old time's sake, you congratulate yourself. You look at the six-pack in your grocery bag. It winks back.

You feel a genuine gratitude for the rental carts in airport concourses.

For men and women who are 50, the carts are one of the noblest humanitarian innovations of our time. Your running-through-airports days are behind you now; the exertion of hauling your carry-on bags up and down the long corridors is more taxing on you than you care to admit. But for $1 or $1.25 or $1.50, the rental carts make it easy. Like pushing a baby's carriage.

As a business traveler, you don't know how the world would go on without these things. And you ask yourself: Is it possible that they've always been there? That you just never noticed them until recently?

Sort of like the denture-cleanser commercials: always

there, but invisible to you for most of your life until, all of a sudden, they become as compelling as *Casablanca*.

The rewards that mean the most of all, you now understand, are not presented by anyone else.

They come to you during those moments when you are doing something that you know in your heart is absolutely right. It may be something that other people ridicule, or don't comprehend; it may be something that no one else in the world is even aware you're doing. Something you feel fervently about, something that is almost holy in its meaning to you, in the devotion that you bring to it.

And the fact that others don't understand—or will never know you've done this—does not matter at all. At 50, you don't have to announce this or explain it to anyone. You know. Which is all that matters. The best reward.

Other rewards—less significant ones—we give to ourselves without even knowing we're doing it.

On a long reporting trip I took, every day I would see two men of about 50 on their five-mile walk. Two and a half miles one way, two and a half miles back. And I noticed something:

At the end of the first leg of their walk there was a large boulder. Each of the men, when reaching the boulder, touched it with one of his feet.

The men didn't need to do this—it's not as if by touching the boulder their walk became any longer. Maybe one or two inches longer. But they both did it.

One morning—after I had seen them do this for the fourth day in a row—I asked them about it.

"Why do you touch the rock with your feet?" I said.

"What are you talking about?" one of the men said.

I told them what I'd been noticing; told them that they

each touched the boulder before turning around for the walk back toward where they started.

"No, we don't," the second man said. Not unpleasantly; with a smile, as if "No, we don't" meant: "*Do* we?"

It's the systematization of the finish line; the need to affirm even the smallest accomplishments. To tell yourself you've done it. The one little motion—the touching of the boulder, and what it represented—is a symbol of many things. It's a pat on the back, in a silent way; a pat on your own back, the day's intangible trophy. Presented to you. By you.

Speaking of trophies:

I was in a store that sold athletic supplies and sunglasses and swimwear—stuff like that. On one table near the front were all the various suntan lotions and sunscreens, with the now-ubiquitous SPF numbers on them: 45, 30, 15, 8, 6, 4, 2. There were many brands in many varieties of bottles and tubes, all promising to help the sun bless the people who might buy them.

There was one brand of suntan lotion, though, that bore the SPF number 0. The numeral was displayed quite prominently on the bottle—the "0" was huge.

The product, according to the label on the bottles, contained "trophy oil."

That's what it said—this particular suntan product was trophy oil. The trophy being the body of the person who put the oil on.

The people who were 50 and over reacted to this product in a different way than the younger browsers. The younger ones—teenagers, men and women in their 20s and 30s—picked up the trophy-oil bottles and passed them back and forth, intently reading the wording on the labels. They seemed to be considering whether to buy.

The people who were 50, though, laughed. Some of them loudly. They talked to each other about the suntan oil, as if the trophy oil were some brilliant standup comedian who had reduced them to howls of hilarity. "Look at this!" they'd say, brandishing a bottle. "They . . . (howl) . . . call . . . (mirthful wheeze) . . . this . . . (renewed howl) . . . stuff . . . (gasping howl) . . . *trophy oil!*"

The body as a trophy.

To be anointed with expensive display oil, like Turtle Wax on a '56 Thunderbird.

The 50-year-olds guffawed and roared, as if they were watching Soupy Sales. The younger people in the store carried bottles of the trophy oil toward the cashier.

I was in a restaurant/bar on a business trip, and a National Basketball Association game was on the television screen. I went out to the bank of pay telephones to call my office, and there was a man—he had been in the same restaurant—on the next phone.

"I know, Reggie Miller's not hitting yet," the man said into the phone. "But they can't stop him for the entire game."

I made my call; the fellow on the next phone kept talking, loud enough so that I heard what he was saying.

"Remember when we watched them play the Knicks?" he said. "How they stopped him at first, but they couldn't keep him down in the second half? You'll see—he'll start hitting those threes."

The man had a contented look on his face as he heard whatever was being said on the other end of the telephone line.

"You have his basketball card, right?" the man said. "Look on the back. It'll give you his shooting percentages for his whole career."

He was talking to his son. The father had been watching
the NBC telecast here in this restaurant; his son, back in the
town where they lived, was watching the same game. And
this was it—the truest and most lasting value of sports. The
aspect that may be most important about sports, and yet
seldom is mentioned:

Sports as the one thing fathers and sons have always been
able to talk about. Sports as the one—sometimes the only—
thing they have in common. The connective thread between them—the common denominator.

A social commentator once said that the games themselves—even the biggest games—do not, in the end, mean
anything. Big games come and go; the result of the game
that seems so important this year will be forgotten two or
three years from now.

But this ancillary function of sports—sports as a way to
bring generations within the same family together, sports as
something a parent and a child can genuinely care about
together, can talk excitedly to each other about with real
shared interest—is, ultimately, the most priceless part of
the contests and the players and the teams. This amazing
thing that sports does—this giving of parents and children
a common ground to walk upon.

There is much discussion about the huge salaries that
professional athletes are paid, and how no one can be
worth that kind of money. But if in any way the star athletes
can be said to earn their money, it is in this way—a way they
perhaps never even think about. It's in bringing together
people that they, the athletes, will never meet; it's in filling
the minds of fathers and sons, mothers and daughters, with
images and family moments that will stay there for years
and years to come.

You know this at 50; when you were younger you thought
the games themselves were what mattered, but now you

know better. I walked back into the bar. Several minutes later, the man returned, too. He watched the basketball game on the screen near the ceiling. Reggie Miller drove for the basket, and as the man watched him, I knew he was thinking of someone else, someone much smaller.

The rewards of being 50 are sometimes things you once would not have considered rewards at all.

Birdbaths and birdfeeders, to name two. You begin to think of birdbaths and birdfeeders as things that would really be nice for you to have.

One of the most pleasant rewards of all is to bring in the day's mail and see that there is a thank-you note from someone you know.

They used to be called bread-and-butter notes—short, handwritten, personal notes from friends or relatives, telling you they're grateful for the good time you just had together, or the party to which you had invited them, or the remembrance you had sent them.

There exists the possibility that the generation turning 50 may find itself the last one to send these thank-you notes as a matter of course. There are many other ways to say thanks these days—phone message machines, computer mail that is delivered instantly with a tap on a keyboard—and perhaps the day is not far off when those elegant little envelopes in the mail don't arrive so routinely. They are to be valued because they are . . . civilized. You've never received one that didn't make you feel good.

A night on the town—once the reward you were constantly giving yourself for any accomplishment you could conceive of, ranging from landing a new account at work to just getting through the week to Friday—no longer sounds like quite the prize it once did.

A night on the town, you frequently think, is just too exhausting to even consider. A night on the town does not sound like a reward—it sounds like an extension of the punishment. At least it does more often than you really want to admit.

So what is an appealing, impromptu reward these days? What can you give yourself that will fill you with a sense of gratitude for having been so thoughtful to yourself?

A glass of real orange juice will do—ice-cold and just-squeezed.

You have begun to concede that there are very few nights on the town that could give you any more pleasure than that glass of orange juice. A night on the town is glaring lights and high-volume horns and hazy decisions to make at every turn. What you would prefer is a screened-in back porch and the soft and silent late-afternoon breeze. If you can't have that reward right this second, the juice is a meritorious substitute.

Although, on evenings when a night on the town is the option that you do choose, your preferred setting for that night on the town often turns out to be an old suspect for which you have found renewed affection:

A steakhouse.

Dark, with white tablecloths, and big salads with extra portions of blue-cheese dressing. Potatoes with onions mixed in. Drinks in heavy glass tumblers.

Steakhouses, you are beginning to surmise at 50, may be who you are, after all.

At least until you can get back to that glass of orange juice on the back porch.

•   •   •

The rewards, at 50, increasingly derive from giving rewards.

I had a friend, many years ago, whose father owned a carpet-and-drapery store. It wasn't a huge company, not one of the modern superstores, but it did well and was respected in its community.

My friend got married immediately after graduating from college. His dad—who must have been around 50 then, not much older—took a look at the apartment my friend and his bride were planning to rent as their first home. And then the dad carpeted the little apartment wall-to-wall with his finest carpets, hung his most luxurious drapes.

I didn't understand, at the time, why this seemed to matter so much to my friend's father. I think I do now. There is a very short period during your life when you go from being the person who is always needing help to being a person who can give the help. Soon enough, you will once again become the person who needs the help. But for a while—and this stage of your life arrives around 50—you are the one who can be turned to.

On large matters, of course, but even, if you own a drapes-and-carpet store, on matters as seemingly small as that. My friend's dad appeared to swell with pride to be able to do this for his son. The father is dead now; he has been gone for quite some time. But I still remember—remember how good he felt, to be the one his son could count on.

While we're on the wedding motif:

One of the great rewards you can count on at 50 is that everything will get funnier.

In the early 1970s, I attended the wedding of a friend in Washington, D.C. When you're 22 or 23 years old you tend to think that most things are hilarious most of the time. And on this guy's wedding day, those of us who were in the wedding party were walking across the lobby of the hotel where the wedding was being held—I believe it was the Shoreham—wearing our tuxedos. And who comes walking toward us from the other direction but Sonny Bono.

Sonny and Cher apparently were performing in the hotel's showroom. And here's Sonny, by himself, and he sees the groom and the rest of us in our wedding clothes, and he stops to give the groom some advice on marriage. Lighthearted stuff, stuff meant to get a laugh, but still—some guy's wedding day, and Sonny Bono is giving tips.

You'd think that life could become no funnier than that, at least in the Sonny-Bono-appearing-unexpectedly-in-Washington-D.C. department. But in the last several years, of course, Sonny Bono has been a Republican congressman in Washington, D.C. He's not giving wedding tips in the lobby of the Shoreham—he's giving tips on national security and on welfare policy on the floor of the House of Representatives. It does no good to try to invent the funniest moments of life—what really happens will almost always be much better. You think you could invent no more outlandish a notion than Sonny Bono going to your friend's wedding. And then Sonny Bono goes to Congress.

One of the great pleasures you may dream of at 50 is of giving yourself a world without bosses. It's possible—there are all kinds of ways to do it, to figure out how to work for yourself, and this is the time of your life when it feels most feasible.

On the surface, it's a happy, giddy notion, like something out of a 1940s movie—you, jaunty and full of confidence, on your own with no boss to answer to, you against the world.

Yet—in addition to the giddy parts—one of the strongest appeals of being your own boss is based on the absence of something—the absence of a dark and flat voice speaking to you on the phone.

Bosses have the power to change people's lives just by the intonation of their voices on the telephone—or, more specifically, by the total lack of intonation. A boss can phone an employee—any employee—and, merely by saying the employee's name in a little different way than when the boss is full of approval, merely by coating his sentences in a layer of studied lifelessness, can send chills of apprehension through the employee on the other end. It's as subtle and nefarious a tool of bosshood as there is—that capacity all bosses have to speak into a telephone mouthpiece with an utter lack of passion or buoyancy, and thus throw the person whose salary they pay into workplace despair.

So at 50, when you make plans to be your own boss, in addition to the free and unfettered expectations there is the other expectation, of knowing that the dark and lifeless voice of disapprobation will never come.

And the question is:

When you are your own boss, who will provide you with that sometimes necessary voice of disapproval and blame?

You?

When you're on a business trip in the summertime, one of the nicest gifts you can give yourself is to go alone at night to the local baseball park—it doesn't matter if it's major league or minor league—buy a ticket, sit in the stands drinking your beverage of choice and eating peanuts and hot dogs, talk to no one, and think.

If it's a major-league city, the team name on the players' uniforms will take you back to the days when the men whose faces appeared on baseball cards represented the apex of what it was possible to do, where it was possible to go. If it's a minor-league town, the look of the park will fill you with the warmth and sensibility of summers past. The being-alone part of this—a person in a ballpark in a city not your own—is what will give the night its texture.

You can sit there watching the ballplayers and hearing the ballpark sounds, and an interior conversation that reaches into every corner of the narrative of your life will be going on. This is something the likes of which you once thought you would never do—buy a single ticket to sit by yourself and watch teams that mean nothing to you near streets with which you are unfamiliar—but right now, at 50, you do it and when the evening is done you feel momentarily complete.

Even on days when the rewards seem elusive, it's good to keep in mind that they tend to show up at their own pace—but they do show up.

One night not long ago the phone rang, and it was an old friend who lives in another town, laughing as he said hello. He told me to turn the television set on to a specific national cable channel; I did, and there was Phil Silvers playing Sergeant Bilko.

"They've been showing this stuff all night," my friend said. "All these Bilko shows, back-to-back. Look at that!"

I did—I looked at Silvers, as Bilko, berating Duane Doberman and Rupert Ritzik and Dino Paparelli, and my friend, more than a thousand miles away, looked too, and we laughed together, entranced by the timing and the skill and the pure comic talent of Phil Silvers.

Many years before—when I was a young reporter—I had called Silvers, hoping to interview him. I had reached him at his home in California; I had been surprised by how dejected his voice was, how down he sounded.

He explained that he didn't feel like talking; he was well past 50, and his career—at least in his eyes, at least on this day—was at a standstill. He said he couldn't get hired for anything; there were no roles for a man like him any longer. "I'm just sitting here looking at my Emmys," he said, very quietly.

He has since died. And he could never have known that, on this night, two old friends—two old friends who, as boys, had been delighted and moved to yowls of joy by the acting craft of Phil Silvers playing Master Sergeant Ernest Bilko— would be sitting in different parts of the country, connected by a telephone line, watching on two different television sets as that acting craft delighted them anew. Let them laugh together anew, over all the miles and all the years. The laughter and the friendship were a reward for the two old friends, yes—and maybe it should also be considered as a reward deferred, but a reward nevertheless, for the man who gave them the laughter.

And a lesson about not counting yourself out. You never know who'll appreciate you. Or when.

Amid the tank tops, cut-off jeans, muscle shirts and short shorts on a typical commercial airline flight, you often notice that you are the only passenger who has chosen to wear a coat and tie. The only one—on the whole plane.

It's a conscious choice—a kind of nod to the days when people got dressed up for travel, because . . . well, because that's what people were supposed to do when they traveled. You're not even a person who dresses up much on the ground, but at 50 you make the effort when you fly. You're not quite sure why. But it's not for the other passengers (as if they'd care). It's for you—a way to make the trip feel a little more like what a trip is supposed to be. Or was.

• • •

"A book is your friend."

Who would ever have guessed that an old slogan like that—words off posters on worn-cork bulletin boards in public libraries, words spoken to classes of students by school librarians—would turn out to mean exactly what it says?

At 50 you are finding out—even in an era said to be defined by megabyte technology and five-hundred-channel video capability and computer data zipping instantaneously from continent to continent—that books, more and more, are what mean the most to you. More than moving images; more than breaking news; more than full-definition audio.

All of those are a part of your life now; all are part of your daily menu. But a book whispers; a book whispers in your ear and becomes a part of you like nothing else you've ever found. There have been predictions that the reading of books, as an avocation shared by the masses, will one of these days disappear; that the reading of books will eventually be little more than a niche activity, like doing needlepoint or playing around with a shortwave radio. People will still do it, or so those predictions go; it's just that the vast majority of people won't.

Perhaps. Perhaps not. But the one thing you're sure of is that if books do end up losing their importance, it won't be in your lifetime. Not in the lifetime of the people who are now turning 50. The people who know a friend when they see one.

When you're 30 or 35 or 40, you might have the impulse to match careers with people, or to match money—to silently compare how you're doing with how they're doing.

Now, though, you realize that the only thing really worth comparing is contentment. Which is not visible on an office organization chart, not measurable in a bank account. And if you're lagging behind, it's much harder to catch up. Or figure out how to.

But, you are certain, worth the effort.

And when you see a person of 50 whistling as he walks—the kind of thing that would drive you crazy if you heard it from the next desk at the office—it strikes you as the ultimate sign of stability. It doesn't make you think the person's odd at all. You see him whistling away, and you ask yourself why you never do.

One night you'll be sitting around the house, deciding whether to make yourself a tuna fish sandwich or just to have a cup of soup.

And instead you'll have a Milky Way and three beers.

It will be a conscious decision. Based on this:

Yes, you know the tuna sandwich is better for you. Yes, you know that if you make yourself the soup, there will be nothing for you to regret the next day.

But then you consider: If at this juncture in your life you can't have the candy bar and the beer, then when can you? If, after fifty years of everything you have gone through, you can't eat and drink some stuff that tastes terrific but that will not do anything beneficial for you, then what have the fifty years been for? If you can't give yourself this little pleasure, then when does the reward kick in? Exactly how long are you supposed to wait for the reward—and on whose schedule?

It's not that you're going to do this every night. You'll be back to tuna and tomato soup by the next day, or the day after. It isn't even a case of lacking willpower. You have plenty of willpower.

It's more that you've decided to make a small withdrawal from the pleasure bank—that place where you've been saving up for all these years. The account in that bank—or so you feel on certain nights—has been built up to a level where taking a little out won't diminish the balance too much. Your account in the pleasure bank is sufficient that you can withdraw some from time to time.

It's there for the same reason all savings accounts are there—for a rainy day.

You hear yourself saying things like this:

"Listen, I'm 50 years old and I know what I'm talking about . . ."

"I'm 50 years old, and I've been to enough of these meetings that I can tell you exactly what's going to happen . . ."

"You don't have to draw me a map—I'm 50 years old, and I . . ."

You hear a tone of whimsy in your voice as you say these things. The words mean what they mean, but you aren't quite as somber about it as the words themselves might indicate. You're getting kind of a kick out of this—it's new territory, unexplored, and you're trying it out. Every time you think about it—much less say it out loud—it has the potential to make you laugh. It's a good feeling—much better than you ever would have guessed.

When you think about all of this seriously, as you do from time to time, you decide that maybe it's finally time for you to unpack.

You've never quite done it—there are always things at your home and in your office that stay boxed up, kept in crates; when you go on business trips, it has always been a temptation just to leave all your clothes in your suitcase and grab what you need out of there every morning, rather than to move everything into the dresser drawers and closet in the hotel room.

There's something about the idea of unpacking that has long seemed to you to be slightly premature. Something you don't really want to trust yourself to do, because there has always been the chance that you'll be moving on soon, heading for the next place. So why waste the effort? Why go to the trouble of unpacking?

At 50, more and more, you think that it's time.

In every way. In ways that have nothing to do with suitcases or boxes.

To unpack once and for all, to make the decision to settle in. To stay put.

Because, you are finding out, you like the place where you are.

About the Author

Bob Greene's national bestsellers include *Be True to Your School; Hang Time: Days and Dreams with Michael Jordan; Good Morning, Merry Sunshine;* and, with his sister, D. G. Fulford, *To Our Children's Children: Preserving Family Histories for Generations to Come.*

Greene is a syndicated columnist for the *Chicago Tribune;* his column appears in more than two hundred newspapers in the United States, Canada, and Japan. For nine years his "American Beat" was the lead column in *Esquire* magazine; as a broadcast journalist he has served as contributing correspondent for *ABC News Nightline.*

The 50-Year Dash is his sixteenth book. His next—*Chevrolet Summers, Dairy Queen Nights*—will be published in the fall of 1997.